Dumb Things
Smart Christians
Believe

WITHDRAWN

Dumb Things *Smart* Christians Believe

Ten Misbeliefs That Keep Us
From Experiencing God's Grace

Gary Kinnaman

VINE
BOOKS

SERVANT PUBLICATIONS
ANN ARBOR, MICHIGAN

All Scripture quotations, unless otherwise indicated, are taken from the *Holy Bible, New International Version®. NIV®.* © 1973, 1978, 1984 by International Bible Society. Used by permission of Zondervan Publishing House. All rights reserved.

Vine Books is an imprint of Servant Publications especially designed to serve evangelical Christians.

Published by Servant Publications
P.O. Box 8617
Ann Arbor, Michigan 48107

Cover design: Eric Walljasper
Cover illustrations: David Hile, Hile Illustration and Design

99 00 01 10 9 8 7 6 5 4 3 2 1

Printed in the United States of America
ISBN 1-56955-117-0

LIBRARY OF CONGRESS CATALOGING-IN-PUBLICATION DATA

Kinnaman, Gary.
    Dumb things smart Christians believe : ten misbeliefs that keep us from experiencing God's grace / Gary Kinnaman.
        p.   cm.
    Includes bibliographical references.
    ISBN 1-56955-117-0 (alk. paper)
    [1. Christian life.] I. Title.
BV4501.2.K496   1999
248.4—dc21   99-31587
                                                    CIP

Dedication

To Mr. and Mrs. Jeff Culver.
That would be my son-in-law and his new wife,
Shari (Kinnaman) Culver,
who are especially grateful for this book
because it helped pay for their wedding,
January 9, 1999.

Contents

Other books by Gary Kinnaman:

And Signs Shall Follow
The Spirit-Filled Life Study Bible (Acts)
How to Overcome the Darkness
Angels Dark and Light
My Companion Through Grief
Learning to Love the One You Marry

Preface

What you are about to learn has the potential to liberate you. It's mostly about rediscovering the grace of God.

It may also trouble you, because it's not common in the Christian community to think deeply about what we believe. If *what* I say doesn't offend you, *how* I say it might, although it is not my intention to offend anyone. At times my style is off-beat and provocative. People tell me they bring their friends to our church because they think I'm funny. I try, because I think it helps people learn when they hear the same old same old presented in a clever, humorous way. For me, humor is a kind of mental and emotional anesthetic to prepare my listeners for spiritual surgery.

And my style of humor? I'm about 80 percent pastor and 20 percent late-night comedian. My wife jokingly says its 20/80, but honestly, after twenty-seven years of marriage, she doesn't always think I'm so funny. Forgive me, but I find *Far Side* cartoons and *Deep Thoughts* by Jack Handy terribly amusing.

This book is not, in the technical sense, therapeutic. I'm not a psychologist, so it's not like a lot of other good Christian books on self-talk and misbelief management. I'm a pastor with a passion to reach people who are unchurched, mad at church, sick of church, bored with church, and disillusioned with church people.

I also have a passion to teach committed Christian people a thoroughly biblical worldview, not just Bible facts. I've seen how Christians everywhere are "godless" in the sense that they are fully immersed in the secular worldview. They love God, but the way the world thinks has them in its grip. Christians are deeply influenced by popular, nonbiblical notions of God, themselves, and others. This book intends to challenge many of those common myths.

Some Personal Things About Me and Our Church

I've been in full-time church ministry for more than twenty-five years, and I've been married a little longer than that. My wife, Marilyn, and I have three children, all serving God. Two of them are away from home, married and working for Christian organizations.

Our church, Word of Grace, has grown to a weekend attendance of four thousand since its birth in 1980. We have about a thousand people a year make professions of faith in our public services, and we baptize hundreds of them every year. We've planted several other churches in and around the Phoenix area. You can reach us at our Web site, www.wordofgrace.org, where you can order audio and video cassettes as well as other books I've written.

Special Expressions of Appreciation

Some acknowledgments are in order. I am deeply grateful that our governing board and church staff at Word of Grace give me the freedom to write. It's time-consuming, and I consider this book a gift from our church to the larger Christian community. We've prayed for it and over it, that those of you who read it will be measurably blessed. Thanks to Harold Christ, Bob Hittenberger, Chris Wolfard, Dean Hodges, Greg Dille, Larry Greenwald, Andy Jackson, and Penny Jo Budd.

Many thanks to the people at Servant/Vine, who have now published four of my books. Don Cooper and Bert Ghezzi, you have been so affirming and supportive. And, Heidi, I've always enjoyed working with you. You are delightful, and your editorial skills have been most helpful.

Finally, I'd like to express my appreciation to John and Barry French and Mark and Lazette La Pierre at the Community of Living Water Conference and Retreat Center in Cornville, Arizona, where I wrote most of this book. Your friendship and hospitality—and the beauty, solitude, and unique spiritual ambience of your facility—kept me safe and focused.

Gary Kinnaman

Introduction:
Smart Reasons to Read This Book

"Kids say the darn'dest things."

"You don't really believe that, do you?"

"It doesn't take a rocket scientist..."

"Hello-o!"

"Duh!"

It's been pointed out to us many times and in many ways that we've said something really dumb. Most of the time we say these things because we're not really thinking about what we're saying. When we do think about it, of course ... how embarrassing! It makes us feel really foolish, not because we said something stupid, but because we realize that in a moment of stupidity we actually believed what we said.

I'm in Hawaii. No kidding.

Right now I'm looking out my hillside, ocean view window. The weather's perfect in paradise. Light breeze. Blue sky. Deeper blue Pacific framed by coconut palms.

No. I'm not a rich author. I'm here for God, if you can believe that. Somebody has to do it. I'm teaching a week-long discipleship seminar at the University of the Nations, a campus of Youth With A Mission, and working on this book in my free time. Friends from our church are here with me, and last night we had dinner at the historic Kona Inn.

"Five years," the server told us. That's how long he'd worked there.

"Since 1928." That's how long the inn had been there.

"No," he didn't surf or sail outriggers.

After annoying him with one dumb tourist question after another (our goal was to ask no less than fifty a day), I urged him to tell us the dumbest question anybody had ever asked him.

He responded immediately: "Does the water go all the way around this island?"

"You're kidding!" we howled.

The question was so preposterous that none of us could believe someone would be *that* dumb, but he reassured us that we were not double dumb for believing him. Yes, someone had actually asked that question.

Of course, *I've* never believed or said or done anything dumb. Well, hardly ever.

At least not since just an hour ago when I turned left in front of a large No Left Turn sign. Someone waved at me, but I thought he was just being friendly.

Isn't it funny how we yell at the driver in the other car, as if we've never made those same mistakes? *We* never get confused in an unfamiliar part of town. Or drive too slow. Or change lanes without noticing the car in our blind spot. Do we?

Blind spots. Everybody has them.

And that's what's so alarming about believing dumb things.

It's nearly impossible to recognize our own stupidity until it's way too late. And when others point it out to us, our pride camouflages our ignorance.

The apostle Paul wrote, "We know that we all possess knowledge. Knowledge puffs up, but love builds up. The man who thinks he knows something does not yet know as he ought to know" (1 Cor 8:1-2).

I take this to mean that true knowledge is laced with self-awareness and readily acknowledges that what we know is only a fraction of what can be known. The volume of what we know is vastly exceeded by what we don't.

Holy Hang-Ups

Finding out how much we don't know can be downright humiliating, and accepting our personal limitations is just plain painful. That goes for Christians as well as non-Christians. When someone challenges our most cherished beliefs about God or Jesus or the Holy Spirit or heaven and hell or the church or who knows what else, we stiffen up in self-defense.

Why, it can shake the very foundations of our faith! We might even doubt a thing or two, and everyone knows that Christians never have doubts. Right? (Wait ... maybe that's one of those dumb things that smart Christians believe!)

In all fairness, at times Christian people have enormous dif-ficulty thinking through their faith because there's so much at stake. Whatever we believe, it better be right. It could be a matter of life and death, heaven and hell.

But self-doubt in search of truth is very different from the kind of doubt that stems from unbelief. It's not good to doubt God, but it may be very good to doubt what you have always thought about God. You really don't have to be afraid to think twice about what you think about God. Real faith is the evidence of things not seen (see Heb 11:1), and to me that implies some uncertainty, some anxiety, even some doubt somewhere in there.

Doubt is the ants in the pants of faith.

FREDRICK BUECHNER

Stuck on Dumb

Try this little game—it was one of my dad's favorites. Read the following sentence out loud.

How do you say the word *stop?*

(C'mon. Don't be cranky. Play the game. Say the word *stop* to yourself—out loud if you can. If you're with other people, just mouth it: "Stop.")

Now say the word *slot.*

How do you say the word *spot?*

What do you do at a green light?

Did you say, "Stop"? Wrong! You don't stop at a green light—you go!

If it didn't work on you, try it on someone else. Ninety-five out of a hundred people will tell you to stop at a green light. Is that dumb or what?

Not really, because this kind of gag, like many other trick questions and riddles, takes advantage of computer-like processes in your brain. Telling you to pronounce a number of similar words sets up a primitive "program," so when I ask you the last question—"What do you do at a green light?"— the first word that comes to your mind isn't the right one. Most people can't help but make fools of themselves.

The lesson, though, is much broader: it's really easy to think dumb thoughts, and it's really hard not to think them, even when you know they're dumb. Our experiences in life create a reality through which we judge and evaluate everything else that happens to us. I interpret life based on my own life, which is never very objective.

Dragging Out Our Ladders

Did you know that the size of a regulation basketball hoop is approximately twice the diameter of a regulation basketball? That you can put two basketballs side by side into the hoop, and with a little nudge, they will drop through?

C'mon! Can't be!

Lots of people in my church refused to believe this, too. When I shared this bit of meaningless trivia with my congregation to introduce my original sermon series "Dumb Things Smart Christians Believe," some of them could barely concentrate on the rest of my message. They were convinced that a basketball hoop is *much* smaller.

Even when I told them that, when I played high school basketball, our coach dragged out a ladder and two basketballs to show us kids how easy it should be to make a basket.

Even when I had a gym teacher take the witness stand.

Even when I held up a *photograph!* "Those are miniature basketballs in that photo!" someone yelled out.

Well, we all know that a basketball hoop *has to be* much smaller than the diameter of two balls, because that's the way it appears to the average person looking up at an object ten feet above the ground. And we all know that the way things appear to us *must be* reality. My perspective *has to be* correct, right?

It was wild. Sunday afternoon, people from my church in neighborhoods across our city were dragging out their ladders to measure the basketball hoops in their driveways, only to discover, of course, that their pastor was telling them the truth. (It made me wonder what they think about everything else I tell them.)

Actually, this was a brilliant example (if I may say so myself) of the power of commonly held misbeliefs—and how extraordinarily difficult it is for people to change their minds. (Come to think of it, that makes me feel a little hopeless about this book. Oh well, maybe someone out there will listen.)

The only feature common to all mental disorders is the loss of common sense and the compensatory development of a unique private sense of reasoning.

IMMANUEL KANT

Mental health is the ongoing process of dedication to reality at all costs.

M. SCOTT PECK

The mind is its own place, and in itself
Can make a heaven of hell, and a hell of heaven.

JOHN MILTON

I Can't Believe You Really Think That!

Marriage is a lot of things, but certainly a good marriage is a lifelong effort to understand, accept, appreciate, and value the unique viewpoint and opinions of your spouse.

Have you ever stared—or glared—at your spouse in angry disbelief? How could he think that! How could she feel that way! Anybody with any brains at all ... is that dumb or what?

Or maybe, just maybe, *your* perspective is really dumb. Is that even remotely possible?

Hey, I'm pretty smart. I have three graduate degrees. But I've believed some really dumb things too. Just ask my wife. Although I probably won't agree with her.

I'm not a psychologist; I'm a pastor. But I have this theory about wholeness: you are mentally healthy if you can think about what you think, and you are mentally unhealthy to the degree that you are not able to think about what you think—that is, if you are not able to evaluate objectively what you think and feel about things.

Now, we all have trouble with that. It's endemic. But at least one indicator of spiritual and emotional maturity is the ability to do self-analysis.

You don't agree? Well, what about little children? Their reality is whatever they're thinking or feeling at any particular moment. Their perceptions are the center of the universe. If you're young and childish, you can even put a towel over your head and no one will be able to see you.

I know this is difficult for us to face, but as adults we still hide from others and from ourselves. Oh, we're much more sophisticated about it now. When was the last time you tried to get away from someone by throwing a towel over your head? How ridiculous! And yet, how often do we console ourselves by imagining that people can't see right through us when we try to hide from doing something particularly dumb? Even worse, do we think we've mastered the skill of fooling God, too?

In a powerful little book, *The Inflated Self,* author David Myers demonstrates that most of us live a lie and don't want to deal with it. "Time and again," Myers writes, "experiments have revealed that people tend to attribute positive behaviors to themselves and negative behaviors to external factors, enabling them to take credit for their good acts and to deny responsibility for their bad acts."

His most startling example came from a survey of high school seniors. In leadership ability, 70 percent rated themselves "above average," 2 percent "below average." Sixty percent viewed themselves as "above average" in athletic ability, only 6 percent as "below average." In their ability to get along with others, none of the 829,000 students who responded rated themselves "below average," while 60 percent rated themselves in the top 10 percent, and 25 percent saw themselves among the top 1 percent![1]

We all hate to admit it, but the harsh reality is that all of us, regardless of how intelligent we are or how spiritually mature we are, believe dumb things. Even when others try to tell us the truth, we construct elaborate systems of denial to conceal our ignorance. But where does that get us?

Ignorance Is Not Bliss

The irony is that the misbeliefs we try so hard to keep under wraps will destroy us in the end. The dumb things we believe make us miserable.

As a psychologist with the highly acclaimed Minirth-Meier Clinic, Dr. Chris Thurman wrote a book titled *The Lies We Believe: The #1 Cause of Our Unhappiness.* He wrote, "Most of our unhappiness and emotional struggles are caused by the lies we tell ourselves.... Until we identify our lies and replace them with the truth, emotional well-being is impossible."

Did you hear that? Emotional well-being is impossible!

Dr. Thurman went on to say that our lives are like a tape deck, and that what we have playing on that deck has a profound effect on our emotional well-being. If it is primarily truth, well and good. If primarily lies, it has a negative effect on us. But what if it's a mix? "If your mind is an equal mixture of both lies and truth, you will experience more of an up-and-down emotional experience. Both lies and truth want to control your tape deck, and whichever gains that control dictates what your life will be like."[2]

Lies produce emotional misery.
Truth produces emotional health.

CHRIS THURMAN

You will know the truth, and the truth will set you free.

JOHN 8:32

Can You Handle the Truth?

It's the truth: the water goes all the way around every island. Believe it.

It's the truth: a basketball hoop is the diameter of two basketballs. Believe it.

It's the truth: the human heart is deceitful above all things and beyond cure. Nobody can fully know themselves. Believe it.

It's the truth: many of the things you believe about God and yourself may be up for review. Believe it.

The way of a fool seems right to him,
but a wise man listens to advice.

PROVERBS 12:15

....

ONE

Misbelief 1:

God Is Eternal, But Mostly I Worry About What He Thinks of Me Now

> You thought I was altogether like you.
> But I will rebuke you
> and accuse you to your face.
>
> PSALM 50:21

"**M**ommy, what's that in the sky?"

"That's an airplane, dear."

"A 'airpane'?"

"Yes, an airplane. You've seen an airplane before. Remember when we took Grandma to the airport and she flew away in that big plane?"

"Oh." (brief pause) "But how did they make all those people so small?"

All of us have trouble grasping what God is really like. I know I do. The biggest problem, I believe, is our tendency to think that our very big God is a lot like us tiny creatures. Or to think we can fit him and his limitless universe into our micro brains. Or to think that the way we think is the way he thinks.

Instead of thinking and becoming more like God, we drag

God down to our level and make him out to be somebody more like us. Even God complains about this: "You thought I was altogether like you" (Ps 50:21).

What Do We Know About God?

On the other hand, theologians like to say that God is "wholly other," entirely unknowable except in what he chooses to reveal of himself. Listen to Israel's most eccentric prophet, Ezekiel, labor to describe an indescribable God. Pay attention to his vocabulary of vagueness, which I've italicized for emphasis:

"Above the expanse over their [the heavenly beings'] heads was *what looked like* a throne of sapphire, and high above on the throne was a figure *like* that of a man. I saw that from *what appeared to be* his waist up he looked *like* glowing metal, *as if* full of fire, and that from there down he looked *like* fire; and brilliant light surrounded him. *Like the appearance* of a rainbow in the clouds on a rainy day, so was the radiance around him. This was the *appearance* of the *likeness* of the *glory* of the Lord" (Ez 1:26-28).

Notice that Ezekiel didn't see the Lord. He didn't see the *glory* of the Lord either. In fact, he didn't even see the *likeness* of the glory of the Lord. All Ezekiel could see was "the appearance of the likeness of the glory of the Lord." And when he saw it, he adds, "I fell facedown" (v. 28). Ezekiel makes no effort to explain anything. His response is worship, not a treatise.

Whatever human language can tell me about God, it tells me precious little. I can't make a lot of assumptions. If I do, my thoughts about God might be pretty dumb. It's been a human problem since the beginning of time, and Job, the oldest book in the Bible, is an example.

Elihu has just finished filling Job's ears with his "knowledge" of what God is like (six chapters' worth!). At last God grows tired of listening and says something: "Who is this that darkens my counsel with words without knowledge? Brace yourself like a man; I will question you, and you shall answer me.

"Where were you when I laid the earth's foundation? Tell me, if you understand. Who marked off its dimensions? Surely you know! Who stretched a measuring line across it? On what were its footings set, or who laid its cornerstone—while the morning stars sang together and all the angels shouted for joy? …

"Will the one who contends with the Almighty correct him? Let him who accuses God answer him!" (Job 38:1-7; 40:1).

Can you picture the scene? Both men facedown on the ground, Elihu wishing very hard that he had stayed at home and not come to "minister" to Job. In thundering silence, God waits for an answer. His voice barely more than a whisper, Job responds: "I am unworthy—how can I reply to you? I put my hand over my mouth. I spoke once, but I have no answer—twice, but I will say no more" (Job 40:4-5).

Now, that's more like it. But God is not quite done. He still needs to get at the heart of the matter and give Job a vision of who he is and what he is like.

First, God says: "Brace yourself like a man; I will question you, and you shall answer me.

"Would you discredit my justice? Would you condemn me

to justify yourself?" (Job 40:7-8).

Then Job replies: "I know that you can do all things; no plan of yours can be thwarted. You asked, 'Who is this that obscures my counsel without knowledge?' Surely I spoke of things I did not understand, things too wonderful for me to know.

"You said, 'Listen now, and I will speak; I will question you, and you shall answer me.' My ears had heard of you but now my eyes have seen you. Therefore I despise myself and repent in dust and ashes" (Job 42:2-6).

It's encouraging to know that misguided thoughts about God are as old as Job. Godly, smart people have believed dumb things about God for thousands of years.

So, What Is God Really Like?

What we can know about God is what he makes known to us—through Scripture and through what he has revealed to us in his Son, Jesus Christ. To think less or to imagine more is mental idolatry. In his classic work *The Knowledge of the Holy*, A.W. Tozer wrote, "What comes to our minds when we think about God is the most important thing about us…. Humankind's spiritual history will positively demonstrate that no religion has ever been greater than its idea of God. Worship is pure or base as the worshiper entertains high or low thoughts of God….

"Wrong thoughts about God are not only the fountain from which the polluted waters of idolatry flow; they are themselves idolatrous. The idolater simply imagines things about God and acts as if they were true…. Before the Christian Church goes into eclipse anywhere ... she simply gets a wrong answer to the question, 'What is God like?'"[1]

So, what is God like? Using the Bible, Christian theologians commonly answer that question by compiling a list of God's attributes, things that describe what he is like. One generally accepted definition of God goes like this: God is an eternal Being, omnipotent (all-powerful), omnipresent (everywhere present), and omniscient (all-knowing).

This is pretty basic. God is all-knowing; he's eternal. He's not restricted by the time and space boundaries of human life.

I can't imagine any Christian not agreeing with this in principle. And yet many Christians, for all practical purposes, think and act in ways that strongly suggest they think God is *not* eternal and all-knowing. And what we misbelieve about God in this regard can be the source of extraordinary pain and shame.

An example of this is the overwhelming sense of guilt we experience when we do something we swore to ourselves we'd never do again. And you wonder—no, you don't just wonder, you're terrified about—what God thinks of you *now*, as if God is just as surprised as you are that you did what you did.

As if God didn't know it was going to happen!

God Stuck in Time

If it is true that God is stuck in time, if he doesn't know what we are going to do next week and is horrified when he finds out what we did today, then our salvation is day-to-day and time-bound. This misbelief dismantles the assurance of our salvation because daily we have to question if the matter is really settled forever in the heart of *an eternal God.*

Here's how, in one place, the Bible addresses this tension between eternity and time, and how it applies to your walk with God: "By one sacrifice he has made perfect forever those who are being made holy" (Heb 10:14).

The first half of the verse teaches that your salvation is complete. From God's perspective in eternity, the work is done. Through the sacrifice of Jesus you have been "made perfect *forever.*" The second half of the verse, "those who are being made holy," touches on the time dimension of your salvation. Salvation is an eternal moment *and* a process in time—both at once.

The problem for us is that we tend to think about the process in time much more than the assurance of eternity. And worse, we more often let time-related events shape how we think about eternity, rather than let our eternal God shape how we think and feel about time-related events.

When I struggle with this, I jerk myself out of my shame by confessing my sin openly to God, and I remind myself that the eternal God is never shocked by the stupid and sinful things I do. This brings great peace to my troubled soul. Certainly, what I do in the present may affect the rest of my life because there are temporal and sometimes terrible consequences to my behaviors (see Gal 6:7-9) . And yet I know that my eternal relationship with God does not teeter-totter on the ups and downs of my daily life.

Promises, Promises

Remember the infamous incident of Peter and the rooster? Hours before the cock crowed, when Jesus and his disciples were huddled in the Upper Room for the Last Supper, Jesus warned Peter, "Simon, Simon [whenever someone calls your name twice, you know you're in trouble], Satan has asked to sift you as wheat. But I have prayed for you, Simon, that your faith may not fail. And when you have turned back, strengthen your brothers" (Lk 22:31-32).

Full of self-reliance, Peter blurted out, "Lord, I'm ready to go with you to prison and to death" (v. 33).

What we have playing out here is a common distortion of the grace of God, the false idea that God really doesn't help the helpless. God only helps those who help themselves. On the one hand, Jesus promised Peter that his faith wouldn't fail. Why? Because of Peter's promise and effort? No! Jesus had already anticipated Peter's personal future (remember, our eternal God is never surprised) and had prayed specifically that Peter's faith wouldn't fail. Grace, all grace, nothing but grace.

In contrast, Peter stood up for himself: "Even if all fall away on account of you, I never will" (Mt 26:33). Never? You'll *never* do that, Peter?

Have you ever made a promise to God like that? Are you going to keep that promise with your whole heart and soul and mind? And what if you don't? What's the God of eternity going to think about you then? And if you do manage to keep your promise, are you going to take credit for it? Will you make quick judgments about people in your life who don't keep *their* promises? Are you better than they are?

Was Peter better than all the other disciples? I think he thought so: "Even if all fall away on account of you, I never will." If it had worked out Peter's way, he could have been pretty proud of himself. But within a few hours he was feeling like a real jerk. He did exactly what he promised he would never do.

Been there. Done that.

Do you think Peter *felt* like his faith failed? Do you think it crossed his mind, *I wonder what Jesus thinks of me now!* Whimper, whimper.

And what about all the people who heard him cursing? Did it seem to them that his faith failed? No doubt.

But tell me, in the end did Peter's faith fail? No! Why? Because that's what Jesus prayed. God's grace was sustaining Peter, not his own self-effort.

The Fruit of Personal Failure

Not only did Jesus know and predict Peter's denial, but he even suggested that his disciple's humiliating failure would be a wonderful example to others. "When you have turned back," Jesus added, "strengthen your brothers" (Lk 22:32).

How is it humanly possible to strengthen and encourage others right after you've made an utter fool of yourself? It's not. That is, it's not *humanly* possible. It's not humanly possible for you to do a lot of things, but "what is impossible with men is possible with God" (Lk 18:27).

The profound lesson here is that Peter's testimony had absolutely nothing to do with anything human. When you encourage somebody out of your own personal success, you're teaching them law and self-efforts, not grace. And if they fail, it puffs you up and puts them down.

In his best-selling book *Grace Walk*, Steve McVey calls this a "vicious cycle, moving from motivation to condemnation to rededication."[2] And you think it all depends on you. Sure, God's there to help you, but you believe it's your effort that counts in the end.

But when you keep the faith in spite of yourself, like Peter, your personal story is not about you. It's about God working in your life. God, all God, and nothing but God.

Before the rooster crowed three times, Peter could talk about how his faith wouldn't fail. "I'll keep the faith," he assured Jesus, "even if it kills me." After the cock crowed, Peter could only talk about God. Peter failed miserably, but in the end his faith didn't fail because Jesus prayed for him.

So, do you consider yourself to be a pretty good Christian? Why do you suppose that is? Do you look down on others because they are not living up to your standards? Really, now, are you living up to God's? Are you, in the words of my friend Dean Sherman, "doing all the right things at all the right times for all the right reasons"?

Or do you consider yourself a pretty good failure? How does that make you feel? What does the eternal God think of you *now*? Is there any hope?

The Peter Principle

Peter's personal problem illustrates the core principle of grace: God always cares more about you than you will ever care about him, and he'll never let that come between you.

This is Paul's theme in Romans 8, perhaps the most important chapter in the whole Bible. Indeed, all Scripture is inspired by the Holy Spirit and is profitable for instruction in righteousness (see 2 Tim 3:16), but what the Bible says about grace has to be our starting point for understanding everything else. This is the whole point of the Letter to the Hebrews, which teaches us that the Old Testament of the law and human effort can only be understood in the light of the "better covenant," the New Testament of grace.

Just as Jesus prayed for Peter, "in the same way, the Spirit helps us in our weakness," writes Paul in Romans 8:26. God doesn't help those who help themselves. He helps the helpless, because "we do not know what we ought to pray for, but the Spirit himself intercedes for us with groans that words cannot express."[3] Furthermore, "the Spirit intercedes for the saints in accordance with God's will" (v. 27). And that's the only reason we can be absolutely certain that "in all things God works for the good of those who love him, who have been called according to his purpose" (v. 28).

Peter's faith didn't fail, because Jesus was praying for him. Your faith, even though at times it looks like it might be slipping, won't fail either, because the Holy Spirit is standing by you in your weakness. I'm sure, then, that everything will work together for good, even my Peter-like failures, because

God is determined to fulfill his purposes in my life.

This is why Paul opens a big can of worms in the next couple of verses: "For those God foreknew he also predestined to be conformed to the likeness of his Son, that he might be the firstborn among many brothers. And those he predestined, he also called; those he called, he also justified; those he justified, he also glorified" (vv. 29-30).

Without getting into all the ins and outs of foreknowledge and predestination, let me just say that all five of the power words in this text—"foreknew," "predestined," "called," "justified," "glorified"—are in the past tense.

As a Christian, regardless of what I can't understand about mysterious things like foreknowledge and predestination, I can at least grasp this: from my time-bound perspective, those are all things that happened in "eternity past." My glorification, though, is in "eternity future." If that's true, why would Paul put that word "glorified" into the past tense too? Because from the point of view of the eternal God, it's all done. If you're a Christian, from God's point of view you are already glorified.

God isn't sitting there on his throne, wringing his hands and wondering what is going to come of you. Those five "power words" are like spokes on a wheel, and when God turns the wheel of his plan for your life, all the spokes turn together, at the same time. ("Time"? There I go again, trying to explain eternity on my terms.)

Paul's point in all this: God is eternal. Believe it and live like it's true. Your fragment of failure in your moment of time will not derail his eternal purposes for your life. But sadly, we more often let time-related events shape how we think about eternity than let the eternal God and his eternal, unchanging plans for us determine how we think and feel about time-related events.

Brain Cramps for God

I'm a Bible believer. I just accept at face value what the Bible says in Romans 8. Can you? Are you willing to allow the Word of God to challenge your assumptions? Are you more willing to believe what God says about himself than what you think God *should* say about himself?

Tell me, is God eternal? Yes.

Does Romans 8 teach that? Yes.

Does it have huge implications for the way we understand eternal salvation? Yes.

Does it mean I can come to Jesus with my weary and heavy-burdened soul and find rest? Yes.

Is it difficult to understand? Not terribly.

Is it difficult to accept? Yes, it can be. Many people stumble over this.

Why? Because we're stuck in time and lost in space. We have little or no capacity to understand eternity, even though we readily confess a belief in an eternal God.

So, can we figure it all out? No.

If we can't figure it out, if it all doesn't fit with everything else we think, if it seems illogical, does that make it untrue? A thousand times, no!

"What, then, shall we say in response to this? If God is for us, who can be against us? He who did not spare his own Son, but gave him up for us all—how will he not also, along with him, graciously give us all things? Who will bring any charge against those whom God has chosen? It is God who justifies. Who is he that condemns? Christ Jesus, who died—more than that, who was raised to life—is at the right hand of God and is also interceding for us" (Rom 8:31-34).

You're worried about what God thinks of you now? So what's Jesus doing for you right now? He's interceding for you right now. Right now while you're trying to figure out in your head what all this means to you.

That's why Paul can't contain himself: "Who shall separate us from the love of Christ? Shall trouble or hardship or persecution or famine or nakedness or danger or sword? ... No, in all these things we are more than conquerors through him who loved us. For I am convinced that neither death nor life, neither angels nor demons, neither the present nor the future, nor any powers, neither height nor depth, nor anything else in all creation, will be able to separate us from the love of God that is in Christ Jesus our Lord" (Rom 8:35-39).

You have a choice. You can choose what to believe. It won't change God, but it will sure change the way you relate to God and others. God will not change the way he feels about you, even if you believe wrong things about him. But if you believe wrong things about God, it will certainly change the way you feel about him. That's why I've subtitled this book, "Ten Misbeliefs That Keep Us From Experiencing God's Grace."

I've chosen to believe what Paul has written in Romans 8. I am convinced that nothing will separate me from the love of God in Christ Jesus, who is in me and praying for me right now. I've decided to let the eternal God and his timeless purposes for me determine what I believe and how I feel about my day-to-day life.

Eternal God: Come into my puny world and water the seeds of my hours and days. Help me to be constantly open to enlarging my vision of who you are and how you work. I trust you to reveal yourself to me, one mystery at a time. As I live in the present, make me mindful that the future never holds any surprises for you. Amen.

....

TWO

Misbelief 2:

God Is Nit-Picking and Short-Tempered

You blind guides! You strain out a gnat but swallow a camel.

MATTHEW 23:24

Overheard at a Monday morning women's Bible study in a church far, far away....

"Did you see the getup she wore to church on Sunday?"

"I know! What was she thinking? Standing up there, crooning into the mike with that canned music, wearing those tacky purple hose! She looked like one of the California Raisins!"

"She *is* our new pastor's wife ... maybe someone should just talk to her privately."

"Someone has to say something. What must God think of his house being turned into a three-ring circus?"

This may come as a shock to you, but here goes: God is not one to split hairs. He isn't always looking over your shoulder, waiting to convict you on some religious technicality. On the contrary. Our God is "a compassionate and gracious God, slow to anger, abounding in love and faithfulness" (Ps 86:15). Not narrow-minded and petty in the least!

Now, you may think God must be like this because so many Christians are, well, narrow-minded, nit-picking, and petty. Not you, of course, and certainly not me. Just all those other Christians we know!

Undoubtedly, Jesus had this problem in mind when he used the now-famous imagery of the mote and the beam. "Don't be nit-picking about the speck in your brother's eye," Jesus said, "when you have a log in your own" (see Mt 7:3-5).

Where this dumb thing comes from, of course, is every Christian's smart compulsion about the truth. Jesus, after all, is the way, *the truth*, and the life. And the church, Paul reminds us, is "the pillar and foundation of the truth" (1 Tim 3:15).

It's Time to Speak the Truth!

It's the truth! Wars have been waged for it. Followers of Jesus have died for it. Whole Christian movements, and later entire denominations, have started up as a result of it. Theologians have argued about it, and churches have split in two or three over it. *It's the truth, and you'd better believe it!* Well, at least it's what I *think* is true, and I know that what I think must be true.

Don't get me wrong. I fully understand that a careful definition of the truth isn't just important; it's essential. Yet when the apostle Paul commands us to "speak the truth," he adds a not-so-little caveat: "in love" (see Eph 4:15). Tell me, then, is there something about truth that needs to be tempered?

As Christians we can really get caught up in "spiritual technicalities." On more than one occasion, for example, I've been asked a question that goes something like this: "I've been taught that we are supposed to pray to the Father in the name of Jesus and in the power of the Holy Spirit. Is it OK, then, to pray directly to the Holy Spirit?"[1]

See what I mean? Nit-picking! My answer has always been, simply, "Yes, it's OK for you to pray to the Holy Spirit." What I would like to say, though, is "Of course not! If you pray to the Holy Spirit, God could never figure that one out!"

We dare not tamper with truth, but we can temper it. I'm quite sure this is what Paul means in 1 Corinthians 13:2: "If I have the gift of prophecy and can fathom all mysteries [fathom *that!*] and all knowledge [that's a lot of truth!] ... but have not love, I am nothing."

The Truth About Truth

Truth is about boundaries established by God, like "Thou shalt" and "Thou shalt not," and the consequences of going outside those boundaries. But here's the problem: boundaries translate into rules, and for many people, rules are more important than the truths on which they're based.

Every year our church has a hugely successful social event in February, our Sweetheart Banquet. It's so popular now that we have to use the largest hotel ballroom in the city. It wasn't always that way, though. We used to do the dinner in our cramped fellowship hall, which would comfortably accommodate about three hundred.

A few years ago, when we were still serving the dinner on

site, I was told by someone on our staff that all the tickets were already sold out—for 150—and we had a waiting list. I was puzzled. "We can seat up to 300, but we are limiting ticket sales to 150? What's the problem?" I asked innocently.

"We only have tablecloths for 150," I was told.

I couldn't believe it! I reacted in a not very pastorlike way. "Then buy or rent more tablecloths, dummy!" (I didn't actually say "dummy," but it sure did pass through my brain!)

It might seem strange to you that anyone could get so bogged down by something as small as tablecloths. But then, you have issues, too, don't you? And boundaries? And rules? Think of the last time you had a family argument. Would your best friends agree that the issues you fight about are important enough to put your friendship, or even your marriage, at risk? Or what about people at work? On the freeway? I mean, is it really worth killing someone over a traffic violation? It happens.

Sometimes we can be so right that we're wrong. God, I believe, is not nearly as concerned as his children are about who's right. He's mostly concerned about who has the right attitude. And when it comes to raising your children, you probably feel pretty much the same way. "I don't care who's right, who started it, or what you're fighting about! Just get along!"

Tithing Breath Mints and Dill Pickles

One of the most troubling things we Christians do is use God to justify our pettiness. That's what some overly religious people, called the Pharisees, did at the time of Jesus.

Taken out of context, the detailed laws of sacrifice in Leviticus can really feed our misbeliefs about God. Our understanding of God must be formed not only through what we read in the law of the Old Testament but also through what has been revealed to us in the New Testament through his Son, Jesus. The scribes and Pharisees got caught up in the rules and details of religion. Jesus, on the other hand, demonstrated that there is a right and a wrong way to do things, even when it comes to giving back to God.

"Woe to you, teachers of the law and Pharisees, you hypocrites!" Jesus announced loudly. "You give a tenth of your spices—mint, dill and cummin. But you have neglected the more important matters of the law—justice, mercy and faithfulness. You should have practiced the latter, without neglecting the former. You blind guides! You strain out a gnat but swallow a camel" (Mt 23:23-24).

There it is in a nutshell. You can be theologically precise and religiously compulsive about obeying the rules—and miss the whole point.

I do believe in tithing, giving 10 percent of my income to God's work. I've tithed since I was a kid, and I teach the principle of the tithe every year in a preaching series I do on God and money. So a fairly high percentage of our congregation tithes. And because people tithe *exactly* 10 percent, we receive checks for odd amounts, like $62.12 or $17.81—the kind of down-to-the-penny checks you write to pay your bills. Technical!

"Round it up!" I shouted (with a smile) one Sunday morning. "Give our church business office a break. If you can't round it up, round it down. God won't take your job away from you, or stop blessing you somehow, if you give him twelve cents less than an exact tithe."

Again, it's all a question of attitude. I know Christians who tithe right down to the cent but who will walk out of church forever if they don't like where the usher is seating them. Talk about gnat-straining!

Smoking Camels

What do you think? Is swallowing camels worse than smoking them?

Whoa, what's that guy saying?

Smoking, of course, has been proven to be a terribly dangerous addiction. The warning is on every cigarette package. I don't smoke, and I don't recommend it for anyone else, but think about how smoking, in many places, has become a *religious* issue. Years ago I was told privately by the pastor of a small church—minutes before I preached in his service—to be sure to make a comment or two about the evils of tobacco. A woman in his church, one of his regular attendees, was a smoker, he told me.

Is smoking unhealthy? Yes! But so is fast food—and myriads of other things Christians consume without an ounce of guilt. That's one of the problems of living by technicalities. Legalism always has loopholes. You just can't write enough rules to cover all the possible ways to break those rules.

Take the Sabbath, for example. Jesus healed people on the

Sabbath, and he did it to make a point all the rules for Sabbath observance in the religious community, many of which had no basis in God's law, were obscuring the real meaning of the Sabbath. Unfortunately, a lot of the people Jesus tried to reach never got the point. (That makes me feel a whole lot better about my ministry. If Jesus couldn't get through, I probably won't get through to everybody either!)

But for those who are ready for good news, who are open to looking at things differently, grace-based Christianity is utterly liberating. Jesus said it this way: "You will know the truth, and the truth will set you free" (Jn 8:32). And when we are set free by the truth, we are free indeed!

Now, About Those Purple Hose ...

"Don't pick on people, jump on their failures, criticize their faults—unless, of course, you want the same treatment. That critical spirit has a way of boomeranging. It's easy to see a smudge on your neighbor's face and be oblivious to the ugly sneer on your own. Do you have the nerve to say, 'Let me wash your face for you,' when your own face is distorted by contempt? It's this whole traveling road-show mentality all over again, playing a holier-than-thou part instead of just living your part. Wipe that ugly sneer off your own face, and you might be fit to offer a washcloth to your neighbor" (Mt 7:1-5, THE MESSAGE).

Got to Keep the Rules

No sitting on the fence! If God said it, you'd better believe it. So don't talk to me about this anymore, because I'm right and you're wrong. And God always takes sides with those who are right, or who are *most* right.

Or does he?

Many people make the unfortunate assumption that, because absolute truth exists, everything in life is either right or wrong, black or white. No gray areas.

I contend, however, that life is *mostly* gray. No, I'm not a moral relativist. I do believe, though, that we live in a very complex world, and spiritual maturity is the ability to recognize and live with ambiguity. Not everything fits neatly into my worldview.

Petty people can't live with a big God, but mostly they can't live with other people, because they just can't make all the people around them fit into their categories. That was the way with the petty religious people who hounded Jesus until the day he died. In fact, they killed him because he kept breaking all their petty rules. Jesus confronted them: "John the Baptist came neither eating bread nor drinking wine, and you say, 'He has a demon.' The Son of Man came eating and drinking, and you say, 'Here is a glutton and a drunkard, a friend of tax collectors and "sinners"'" (Lk 7:33-34).

Lizards on the Farm

If you haven't figured it out yet, I have an offbeat way of look-ing at life. No, my kids aren't dysfunctional as a result, but I did mess with their minds from time to time. Like when I would sing to them, "Old MacDonald had a farm, E-I-E-I-O. And on his farm he had some lizards, E-I-E-I-O."

"No lizards on the farm! No lizards on the farm!" was my kids' dismayed response. We all know that Old MacDonald didn't have any lizards on that farm, don't we? Unless, of course, he lived in Arizona, like we do. We have lizards and rattlesnakes and scorpions and tarantulas on our farms.

"No!"

"Yeah!"

Of course, we also have greenbelts and river valleys! Nearly one-third of our state is pine forest. Granted, it's not what most people think of when they think of Arizona. Some years ago, when my great-aunt came to visit us from Ohio, she brought along extra toothpaste and cosmetics, because every-one back East knows Arizona is the Wild West. I guess she wasn't even sure if we had drugstores.

Well, Arizona has drugstores. And Wal-Mart. And Saks Fifth Avenue. And grassy spruce- and aspen-rimmed meadows ablaze with flowers sprinkled by summer rains. God's creation is full of wild surprises, and not everything is the way you think it is.

Everything is not black and white. Or even gray. Our world is full of vibrant color. Few things in life are totally simple. If you're not convinced, a good place to start looking is the Ten

Commandments: "Honor your father and mother, so that you may live long in the land the Lord your God is giving you" (Ex 20:12). Pretty clear, right? Yes, children should love, honor, respect, and obey their parents.

But how does a daughter show love and honor to a dad who is sexually abusing her? How does a son respect and honor a parent whose infidelities are tearing apart the family? How does the commandment apply in those cases?

And what about the next commandment: "You shall not murder" (v. 13). Everyone (with the exception of sociopaths) believes that this commandment must be vigorously upheld. Murderers go to prison. Sometimes we even put them to death (putting to death a murderer is not called murder), and even though we know we shouldn't, deep down inside we feel good when the executioner gives a lethal injection to a really dastardly human being.

Just last week we had a drive-by shooting that made huge headlines. A group of kids, walking together in a good and decent neighborhood, exchanged a friendly wave with some other kids waving in a passing car. Except the people in the car weren't waving. It was a gang sign, and the unsuspecting teens who waved back were greeted by a shotgun blast that killed two of them right there on the spot.

Without a hint of remorse, the fifteen-year-old perpetrator defended himself, "They dissed [disrespected] me."

So what about capital punishment for this guy? What about capital punishment for any guy? What about war? What about killing thousands of Iraqis in Desert Storm? Or Serbs in Yugoslavia? Was that murder, or was that necessary?

Really, at this point I'm not suggesting any answers. Whole books have been written on each of these issues. What I am trying to show you, however, is that it hurts to think about all this stuff, because we know there are no easy answers.

Joseph and His Technicolor Temptation

Some things I know: Murder is wrong. Theft is wrong. Adultery is wrong. Child abuse is wrong. And for a litany of other rights and wrongs in the New Testament, check out Ephesians 4:17–5:20. In the Old Testament, aside from the Ten Commandments of course, the story of Joseph is as good an example of right and wrong as you can find.

Joseph, one of a dozen brothers, was the favorite son of Jacob. Sold into slavery by his jealous brothers, Joseph eventually found himself in Egypt working as the house master of a rich man, Potiphar, who had a sensual wife. "Now Joseph was well-built and handsome," the Bible describes him, "and after a while his master's wife took notice of Joseph and said, 'Come to bed with me.'

"But he refused. 'With me in charge,' he told her, 'my master does not concern himself with anything in the house.... How then could I do such a wicked thing and sin against God?'" (Gn 39:6-9).

His moral convictions cost Joseph his job and nearly his life, but no one would doubt that he did the right thing. Some things are worth dying for. There *are* moral absolutes. But there are also moral dilemmas. A lesser-known Old Testament narrative demonstrates the complexity of some moral choices, how right and wrong is not always so black and white.

Second Kings 5 records the account of Elisha and Naaman, the commander of the heathen king of Aram. "He was a valiant soldier," the Bible says, "but he had leprosy" (v. 1). Hearing about the prophet Elisha, Naaman sought him out for prayer. By messenger, Elisha gave him simple instructions: "Go, wash yourself seven times in the Jordan, and your flesh will be restored" (v. 10).

Naaman was incensed. Elisha's demand assaulted his pride. How could the man of God ask him to bathe in the dirty Jordan? "Are not Abana and Pharpar, the rivers of Damascus, better than any of the waters of Israel?" he objected. "Couldn't I wash in them and be cleansed?" (v. 12). So he turned and went off in a rage, the Bible reports.

Fortunately, his wise servant talked him out of his tantrum, and when Naaman dipped himself seven times in the Jordan, as Elisha had instructed, God miraculously healed him. Returning to Elisha to give thanks, he posed an imponderable: "Your servant will never again make burnt offerings and sacrifice to any other god but the Lord. But may the Lord forgive your servant for this one thing: When my master enters the temple of Rimmon to bow down and he is leaning on my arm and I bow there also—when I bow down in the temple of Rimmon [a pagan god!], may the Lord forgive your servant for this" (vv. 17-18).

What would you tell him? That he was compromising his convictions? Not Elisha, who offered the man amazing grace in his moral dilemma: "Go in peace," Elisha said (v. 19).

It's a risk for me to retell this story, because somebody out there is going to use it as biblical excuse for compromise. But it's worth the risk because it so clearly shows how, even in the Bible, things are not always so black and white. Some things are morally complex.

For the Love of Women

I have a friend who is the senior pastor of a huge church in Nigeria, West Africa. Paganism is rampant in his city, and outside the church, polygamy is socially tolerable. So not infrequently one of those modern-day Solomons becomes a Christian. What to do?

American missionaries, he told me, would insist that the polygamist put away all but one wife—immediately. But that would create even more problems, my friend told me. You see, in his cultural setting, any wife put out of a polygamous relationship becomes street trash. So a lengthy and delicate process is necessary for men with multiple wives to make a transition to monogamy.

Here's another one: beer. Not the drink of choice of many good American Christians. But in Europe? In Germany? Another good friend, a missionary to Europe for many years, told me of a conversation he'd had with a German pastor. (Yes, in case you're wondering, the German pastor was born again!) With his hand in a white-knuckle grip on his stein, he was literally crying tears in his beer about how American Christian women indulged themselves in facial makeup and wore pants.

These things are very offensive to European Christians, while a deep mug of skunky brew is not offensive in the least.

So, Tell Me What's Really Wrong

Am I suggesting that drinking is right and makeup is wrong? Now, don't get technical on me and miss the point. You might end up being just like the people who were swallowing camels.

So you protest, "What's right and what's wrong? Aren't we just talking about moral relativism?"

Nope, we're talking about moral *complexities* and moral *dilemmas.* In seminary it's called ethics, the study of right and wrong when it's not self-evident what's right and wrong.

Hear me out, please. To repeat what I said earlier, there are some things I know: Murder is wrong. Theft is wrong. Adultery is wrong. Child abuse is wrong. Drunkenness and overeating are wrong.

But I'm also concerned that Christians are not thoughtful about the more complex moral issues of life—and are too willing to jump to judgments. Good, smart Christians are often more rules-oriented than grace-based, too. As for me, even when I've done something clearly wrong, I am grateful for God's persistent mercy and forgiveness. "He does not treat us as our sins deserve or repay us according to our iniquities. For as high as the heavens are above the earth, so great is his love for those who fear him" (Ps 103:10-11).

We need this level of love for one another, too: "Be kind and compassionate to one another, forgiving each other just as in

Christ God forgave you" (Eph 4:32). The big problem, you see, is that when people think God is nit-picking, they start picking on each other. But when you know God fully and you experience his forgiveness deeply, you'll love others unconditionally.

I've come to the unwavering conviction that the grace of God working *in* me—not rules and rule-driven people working *on* me—brings about change in my life. So I'm appealing to you. If you have to speak the truth, speak it in love. Listen deeply and love intensely before slicing up someone's soul with a razor's edge of simplistic advice.

....

Merciful God: Help me to reflect your compassion to the world around me. By your Spirit, make me sensitive to the needs of others, including the need for mercy and a good example. May I seek righteousness, not simply rightness. Thank you for grace, which you give me so freely each day. Amen.

....

....

THREE

Misbelief 3:

God Grades on a Curve
(The Better You Are, the Bigger the Blessing)

> When a man works, his wages are not credited to
> him as a gift, but as an obligation.
>
> ROMANS 4:4

*O*verheard *after Sunday school in a church far, far away....*

"Mom, Miss Mitchell says that when we go to heaven we'll get rewards for the good stuff we did. Is that right?"

"Why, I suppose so."

"So if I clean my plate and don't hit my sister every day, God will give me a motorcycle?"

"I don't think it works quite like that, Johnny...."

"And if you give money and teach the Sunday school and go to committee meetings and volunteer at the soup kitchen and coach the church softball team, you must get something really great! What do you get?"

"I've been there, Johnny. Mostly, you just get tired."

God helps those who help themselves.

Do you believe it? If so, you're not alone. According to a

recent study by the Barna Research Group, a majority of Americans—80 percent—believe it's in the Bible.[1] (Surprise! It's not.)

Barna also found that "most Americans believe that spiritual salvation is an outcome to be earned through their good character or behavior. Six out of ten people (57 percent) believe that 'if a person is *generally* good, or does *enough* good things for others during their lives, they will earn a place in heaven.'"[2]

But how do you measure *"generally* good" or *"enough* good"? How much do you need to help yourself before God steps in to help you? A day? A week? Two years? Sixty-three percent of all the days in a two-year period?

At what point does God help? And how much does he help? In equal proportion to your effort? Or do you have to help yourself a minimum of 15 percent of the time? Forty percent of the time?

Does God ever give up helping? At what point? After you've given up for a day? Three days out of ten? Denied him three times before the rooster crows? Three more times *after* the rooster crows?

Is your head spinning yet? If not, brace yourself for the terrible truth: God doesn't grade on the curve. If you want to go to heaven on your own steam, you have to score 100 percent. You have to do all the right things at all the right times for all the right reasons.

Sound impossible? It is. The Bible makes this painfully clear: "Whoever keeps the whole law and yet stumbles at just one point is guilty of breaking all of it. For he who said, 'Do not commit adultery,' also said, 'Do not murder.' If you do not commit adultery but do commit murder, you have become a lawbreaker" (Jas 2:10-11).

Jesus made it even more difficult for the "good person" to go to heaven when he preached his great Sermon on the Mount. His opening remarks have to give all the best religious people in the world an incredible sinking feeling: "I tell you that unless your righteousness surpasses that of the Pharisees and the teachers of the law [those would be the most meticulous keepers of religious rules in the history of religious rules], you will certainly not enter the kingdom of heaven" (Mt 5:20).

Being Good Isn't What It Used to Be

Jesus redefined what everybody thought it meant to be good, to obey the law. For example, to the Pharisees, staying morally pure involved (among other things) having sex only with your wife. But Jesus took it a step further. He taught that adultery, from God's point of view, occurs when a man glances at another woman and just *thinks* about having sex with her. (And since God is the ultimate Judge, his point of view is the only one that matters!)

And murder? According to Jesus, "Do not commit murder" includes keeping your mouth shut when you're really upset with somebody—for example, the guy driving like an idiot on the freeway. "Anyone who says, 'You fool!' will be in danger of the fire of hell" (Mt 5:22).

Yeah, sweet Jesus said that.

If I just call somebody a fool? Is that really such a bad word? I can think of much worse things to say to people. If what you're telling me is true, Jesus, nobody's *going to heaven based on their own goodness!*

Precisely the point.

Nobody's good enough. Nobody can pass the test. Everybody has sinned and falls short of the glory of God (see Rom 3:23). The Greek word for sin in the New Testament, *hamartia,* doesn't mean "doing really dreadful things." *Hamartia* just means "falling short" or "missing the mark."

God is perfect, you see, and for his sake you have to hit the center of the bull's-eye every time. And you have to hit it at a hundred yards. No, actually, after carefully inserting an arrow into the dead center of the target, you have to shoot a second arrow from two hundred yards into the center of the back end of the first arrow. If you don't, you've sinned in the sense of *hamartia.* You've "missed the mark."

By way of illustration, imagine that God is on one side of the Grand Canyon—ten miles wide, one mile deep—and we're all on the other side, trying to jump across. Some will jump a little farther than others. If all of us lined up and jumped at precisely the same moment, Carl Lewis, who won four Olympic gold medals for the long jump, would be the last of us to die.

But we keep trying! We keep putting ourselves back on the curve, jumping to our death by saying dumb little things like "I'm not as bad as *those* people." We're addicted to our self-effort. We keep trying to overcome our own sin.

The Tyranny of Performance Orientation

Sin is doing bad things—yeah, even after we become Christians. We feel awful about it, although our feelings are not always the best indication of the seriousness of the offense. For example, we may feel worse over sin *after* we're born again than before accepting Christ, because we are so much more open to God's Word and sensitive to the Holy Spirit. And our feelings can play tricks on us. When the Holy Spirit reminds us of our sin, the devil tries to turn it into a sense of personal failure and condemnation.

Generally, the more we see our sin, the more terrible we can feel. So to make up for it, we try our best not to do bad things to avoid the pain—and to do good things to feel better about ourselves. So the better we do, the better it makes us feel.

It's enslavement!

Actually, biblically, it's the curse of sin. Not only am I bound by the power of sin because I keep doing the things I hate—and I hate myself for it—but I'm also caught in a dead-end system of performance.

Feeling overwhelmed? Hey, it's the real world of sin and its corresponding curse of performance orientation. Everything is on a curve, and the curve has no mercy. Any deviation from the norm, and you're cursed.

But what's the norm? That's part of the problem. No one knows, and because the curve is so subjective, you never know exactly when somebody isn't going to like you anymore. We've all had friendships end over, well, nothing.

For Christians the questions are different but the principle is the same. Worldly criteria such as "What kind of car do you drive?" (family minivan, business sedan, "midlife crisis special") and "What do you do?" (software consultant, garbage collector, homemaker) are replaced with more "spiritual" standards:

- What church do you go to, and how often do you go?

- How often do you pray in public, and how well?

- Are your children Christians?

- Do you have any character flaws (anger, lust, envy, greed, irritability)?

- How much do you put in the offering plate?

- How many church activities do you support or at least attend?

- How many of your neighbors have you invited to church?

- Do you (choose one): (1) lead a small group, (2) attend a small group faithfully, or (3) run the other way when approached by a small-group leader?

The sad truth is that many Christians believe, deep down, that how other Christians feel about us is a good indication of how God feels about us. Henri Nouwen writes about this in his provocative little book *The Return of the Prodigal Son: A Story of Homecoming*:

"At issue here is the question, 'To whom do I belong? To God or to this world?' Many of my daily preoccupations suggest that I belong more to the world than to God. A little criticism makes me angry and a little rejection makes me depressed. A little praise raises my spirits, and a little success excites me. It takes very little to raise me up or thrust me down…. My life is mostly a struggle for survival: not a holy struggle, but an anxious struggle resulting from the mistaken idea that it is the world that defines me….

"The world says: 'Yes, I love you *if* you are good-looking, intelligent, and wealthy. I love you *if* you have a good education, a good job, and good connections. I love you *if* you produce much, sell much, and buy much.' There are endless 'ifs' hidden in the world's love…. It is a world that fosters addictions because what it offers cannot satisfy the deepest craving of my heart."[3]

So here's the misbelief stated in more thorough terms: God grades on a curve, and so a relationship with him, from start to finish, is based on Jesus plus something. No one can agree what that something is, or how much of it you need.

Utterly Unconditional Grace?

I'm convinced that utterly unconditional grace, which I refer to as "Jesus plus nothing," is one of the most difficult concepts to teach Christians, to teach anyone—even though it's clearly in the Bible—because part of the curse of sin is the overpowering compulsion to keep grading and degrading ourselves and everybody else on the curve.

Paul explained it this way: "All who rely on observing the law are under a curse, for it is written: 'Cursed is everyone who does not continue to do everything written in the Book of the Law'" (Gal 3:10).

"Everything" is a huge word. You can't just be the best

person you can be, or better than most other people. God is perfect, and he sets the standard. That why Paul adds, "Clearly no one is justified before God by the law" (v. 11). So if it's humanly impossible to keep the whole law, then it's humanly impossible to go to heaven. Right?

Danger: No Curves Ahead

Remember, God *doesn't* grade on the curve. You can't sit back and reassure yourself, *I'm a pretty good person,* implying that somehow you are going to make it and others aren't. If you were to make it on your own merits, you'd have to score 100 percent! (Remember the Grand Canyon?)

But the really good news is that God has offered a way out: his Son, Jesus, did what was humanly impossible. For thirty-three years Jesus did all the right things at all the right times for all the right reasons. He scored 100 percent on God's holiness exam.

Then he died, an absolutely perfect sacrifice. He took my sins into himself and suffered the consequences. The Grim Reaper, who was knocking at my door, took the life of Christ instead. Through an inconceivable exchange, all my sin and shame were transferred into Jesus' account, while all his perfection is transferred into mine. The limitless wealth of his perfect righteousness is deposited into the bank of my heart.

Paul wrote, "But now a righteousness from God, apart from the law [that is, my religious efforts], has been made known.... This righteousness from God comes through faith in Jesus

Christ to all who believe" (Rom 3:21-22). Abraham, the father of the Jewish nation, as good a man as you'll find anywhere, wasn't good enough. But Abraham "believed God, and it was credited to him as righteousness" (4:3). In other words, Abraham's faith was like righteousness on credit.

When I'm born again, I get a new nature inside me, the very nature of Jesus himself. Suddenly a human impossibility becomes an immediate, personal reality. In the twinkling of an eye I pass the test of God's perfect standards. With Jesus in me, I can hurtle across the Grand Canyon of sin and death in a single bound. I make the quantum leap from falling way short to being fully accepted by God forever, not because I've lived up to God's standards, but because Jesus did, and he's in my heart. As long as I live, the righteousness of Jesus "on credit" keeps on making up for the righteousness deficit in my life.

"Christ redeemed us from the curse of the law," Paul boasted, "by becoming a curse for us, for it is written: 'Cursed is everyone who is hung on a tree'" (Gal 3:13). Notice: Jesus didn't just redeem us from the curse of sin. He has liberated us from the curse of the law, or to use my term, the curse of the curve, the curse of my relentless self-effort to fulfill the expectations of God.

Grace From Start to Finish

We're saved by grace alone, not by a single good work. It's Jesus plus nothing.

Every Christian knows that!

Oh, do they?

Watch out now, that performance orientation can sneak up on you before you know it! Next thing you know, you're grading yourself on the curve again, *after* you're born again.

You think not?

Let me ask you a few things. Just a few provocative, unnerving questions. What does it mean to be a Christian? Is it *really* Jesus plus nothing? For instance, can you be a Christian and

- smoke?
- drink? (If so, how much? One glass of wine? A six-pack of beer? A six-pack of beer in three hours?)
- watch R-rated movies?
- dishonor your aging parents?
- call somebody a fool?
- lose your patience in line at the bank?
- have an abortion?
- believe in evolution?
- tell racial jokes?

OK, OK. These aren't *good* choices for Christians to make, but if they make them anyway, does that mean they aren't really Christians after all? What if they do them just once? What if they do them over and over? How many times can God put up with a problem before he goes over the edge? What if a Christian is right in the middle of a racial joke and dies before he gets to the punch line? Will he go to heaven?

Is salvation *really* Jesus plus nothing? Is God's grace *really* utterly unconditional? Or is it Jesus plus something? And if it is, what is that "something," and (an even better question) who's going to decide? How about...

- The Pentecostals? Jesus plus speaking in tongues.
- Holiness churches? Jesus plus many things.
- The Catholics? Jesus plus the sacraments.
- The Baptists? Jesus plus regular church and Sunday school attendance.
- The Seventh-Day Adventists? Jesus plus church on Saturday.
- The Mormons? They believe in a very different Jesus plus, plus, plus, plus...

I know. I'm being terribly superficial, and few of these religious persuasions would say outright that you don't have to do any of these things to be saved, but there could be some serious doubt about your relationship with God if you didn't.

So, What's Your Hot Button?

Jesus plus circumcision.

Now, there's a dead issue. Circumcision. But it wasn't dead at all when Paul wrote Galatians. In fact, a careful study of the New Testament suggests that circumcision was probably a more explosive issue in the early church than abortion or evolution is among Christians today. All the first Christians were Jews, and the rite of circumcision was a sign to them of God's covenant with Abraham, which was instituted nearly five hundred years before Moses received the Ten Commandments on Mount Sinai.

Today the issue of circumcision is just an interesting footnote in the history of the early church. It means little or nothing to us. Say the word to yourself: "circumcision." Feel any emotion?

Now say this word: "abortion." Any feelings about that?

How about this sentence: "I just found out that my sister is in a lesbian relationship"?

If you're just sitting there reading this and not feeling a thing, call your next-door neighbor and ask her how she feels about abortion or gay rights. Let the fireworks begin! (I guarantee you won't get nearly the same response over the word "circumcision.")

Not so in the first-century church. The circumcision debate in the early church was volcanic. The Book of Acts reports urban riots over the issue (see Acts 21:27-36). If you don't understand this, Galatians will not make sense to you. This epistle was written to address the inclusion of Jewish religious practices, particularly circumcision, into the new Christian communities. Some Jewish Christians, who became known as Judaizers, were insisting that Gentile Christians had to be circumcised. It was a problem of Jesus plus circumcision. *Jesus plus something.*

How did this make Paul feel? In a word, livid. Writing about the same problem in his Letter to the Philippians, Paul lashes out, "Watch out for those dogs, those men who do evil, those mutilators of the flesh" (Phil 3:2).

Paul's a little more levelheaded in Galatians, but not much. His key thought is perhaps Galatians 2:20-21: "I have been crucified with Christ and I no longer live, but Christ lives in me. The life I live in the body, I live by faith in the Son of God, who loved me and gave himself for me. I do not set aside the grace of God, for if righteousness could be gained through the law, Christ died for nothing!"

Let me reword that: I didn't become a Christian by grace, only to set grace aside after I got saved, because my righteousness did not come to me through my own effort in the first place. Righteousness could never be gained by the law, and if we go back there, we are saying, in effect, that Jesus died for nothing. When Jesus died, if he did everything to make my salvation possible, then my relationship with God is based on Jesus plus nothing. If, on the other hand, I believe that my salvation is based on Jesus plus something, then Jesus died for nothing.

There's no middle road. If I add human effort to my salvation after I get saved, I am watering down the work of Christ on the cross. Jesus didn't just die to help me get saved. Jesus died to save me completely. He saves me from both my past and my future (see Rom 6:5; 8:30, 38) because I am utterly helpless from beginning to end. That's why I need the utterly unconditional grace of God to save me and to sustain my salvation.

Salvation plus something means that Jesus didn't have to die, or that when he died, it was only to purchase part of my salvation, like the beginning part. As we work our way through some of the key points of Paul's Letter to the Galatians, it's really important to keep reminding ourselves that Paul isn't just writing about grace for initial salvation, but grace to keep us saved. And that's what the writer of Hebrews had in mind when he wrote that Jesus is both the author and the finisher of our faith (see Heb 12:2).

Oh, this is so wonderful!

Oh, this is so difficult for us to receive because we are so enslaved by performance orientation, so bound by the curse of the curve. Yes, even *after* we've been saved by grace. But if we are truly saved by grace through faith, we can live by faith, too (see Rom 1:17; Gal 3:11). Count on it: God's grace frees us not only from the "curse of the curve" (performance orientation), but the curse of legalism as well!

Really Mad About You

Well, then, how serious is it to mix a little of Jesus with a little of this and little of that? Look at Galatians 1 and cringe. "I am astonished," writes Paul, "that you are so quickly deserting the one who called you by the grace of Christ and are turning to a different gospel—which is really no gospel at all" (vv. 6-7). That would be Jesus plus circumcision. Don't forget, circumcision was like spiritual gold among the early Jewish Christians.

"Evidently some people are throwing you into confusion and are trying to *pervert* the gospel of Christ" (v. 7). "Pervert"? Strong words, Paul! In fact, in Galatians Paul is more outraged about Jesus plus something than he is about sin. Oh, he comes down hard on sin, too, but his acute passion is for utterly unconditional grace.

Paul continues, "But even if we or an angel from heaven should preach a gospel other than the one we preached to you, let him be eternally condemned! [Eternally condemned? Wow!] As we have already said, so now I say again: If anybody is preaching to you a gospel other than what you accepted, let him be eternally condemned!" (vv. 8-9).

Why would Paul be so inflamed that Christian leaders in the Galatian churches were adding things to the gospel, the utterly good news that grace is utterly unconditional?

First, Jesus plus something, to use Paul's terms, *perverts* the gospel (the New Testament Greek term translated "gospel" means, simply, "good news"). Jesus plus something puts salvation back on the curve. Taking away the "good news" of God's unqualified love in Christ, it throws the responsibility back on you, making relationship with God conditional after all. And that's not "good news." It's not the true "gospel." Paul says it this way: Jesus plus circumcision is "really no gospel at all." Actually, it's really *bad* news. It's a curse.

Second, Jesus plus something ruins relationships. It leads to legalism, which leads to judgmentalism, which leads to rejecting others. Look at Galatians 2:11-14: "When Peter came to Antioch, I opposed him to his face, because he was clearly in the wrong." About what, Paul? Was Peter sinning? Backsliding? Nope. Wilting under the pressure of the Judaizers, Peter had gone spineless in the powerful presence of the dark prince of performance orientation and legalism.

"Before certain men came from James, he used to eat with the Gentiles. But when they arrived, he began to draw back and separate himself from the Gentiles because he was afraid of those who belonged to the circumcision group." Jesus plus something makes us all go back to grading on the curve, and some people just won't make the grade. Like uncircumcised Gentiles. They weren't as good as Peter.

Actually, I find a great deal of consolation in this passage, knowing that even the apostle Peter had trouble mixing grace and works. And so did Barnabas: "The other Jews joined him in his hypocrisy, so that by their hypocrisy even Barnabas was led astray." The name Barnabas means "son of consolation." The man was a peacemaker, but even the nicest people can let legalism take them down.

"When I saw that they were not acting in line with the truth of the gospel [the "good news," Jesus plus nothing]," Paul went on, "I said to Peter in front of them all, 'You are a Jew, yet you live like a Gentile and not like a Jew. How is it, then, that you force Gentiles to follow Jewish customs?'"

OK, So People Can Live Like the Devil?

Too much grace, people warn me, and you're going to give Christians the idea that they can do whatever they want. This objection burps up in one form or another all the time, but only when somebody teaches that grace is utterly unconditional. People leveled the same accusation at Paul:

"Why not say—as we are being slanderously reported as saying—'Let us do evil that good may result'"? (Rom 3:8).

"What shall we say, then? Shall we go on sinning so that grace may increase?" (Rom 6:1).

"What then? Shall we sin because we are not under law but under grace?" (Rom 6:15).

You can disagree with me. You can even dispute the notion of utterly unconditional grace. Many do. But you can't argue about this: it's exactly what Paul is teaching in Galatians and Romans. That he expects these objections is proof of that. If Paul were teaching grace plus something, he would not have had to concern himself with the possibility that some of his readers would misunderstand.

Why, tell me, are there so few pastors and teachers following in the footsteps of Paul? And when Christian leaders do teach us about God's grace, which they do often, why don't more people pop up and dissent? Are we hearing about some kind of *conditional* grace most of the time? I contend that men and women of God are not teaching grace the way Paul did unless people raise the same objections that Paul anticipates from his readers. If grace isn't controversial, then it's probably not utterly unconditional, New Testament grace.

Conditional grace is not nearly so objectionable, you see, because it leaves room for *some* good works. After all, none of us could be *that* bad. Do we react less to the common ideas of slightly conditional grace because they leave the door of performance orientation open just a crack, and performance orientation is so much a part of our psyche?

Yes, Jesus plus nothing flies in the face of a very powerful, godless world system rooted in the fundamental principle of evolution: the survival of the fittest. Under the curse of sin, the whole creation grades on the curve, including every religious system except New Testament, grace-based Christianity. Only the best survive, only the "most spiritual" are blessed. In striking contrast, the utterly unconditional grace of God in Christ is the only place in the universe of science and religion where there's not a trace of the curve. No one is better than anyone else. People either have Jesus in their hearts or they don't.

We have, though, a trace of curveless acceptance in family love. Think about this: *the love that parents have for their children is always different from the love children have for their parents.* Or for one another! Generally, parents love their kids more than kids love their parents—and certainly more than kids love each other. And if it's true of the human family, how much more true must it be of the family of God?

This follows what Paul writes in Romans: "Since we have now been justified by his blood, how much more shall we be saved from God's wrath through him! For if, when we were God's enemies, we were reconciled to him through the death of his Son, how much more, having been reconciled, shall we be saved through his life!" (Rom 5:9-10).

God will always love you more than you love God, and if he loved you before you joined his family, if his love is big enough to get you in, don't you think it's just as big, even bigger, to keep you in? Paul is telling us in Romans 5 that the big hump for God is getting you saved in the first place. After that, it's downhill. But oddly, many smart Christians turn that around. Practically speaking, they make initial salvation easy for God. You know, you've heard it over and over: he'll save you just the way you are. Nothing's too hard for God. No sin is outside his love.

But once a person gets saved—oh, brother—does it ever seem hard for God to finish the task, probably because deep inside we think it's up to us to finish the task. Our problem is that we try to understand God's love from our point of view, like a little child trying to grasp the depth of Mommy's love. But for us to know God's love, we have to believe in what he says about himself, not what we think about him.

Why Do Anything?

Here's the very common objection one more time: If God does it all, why do anything? I will answer that fully in the next chapter. I believe in living for God, loving him with your whole heart and soul and mind, and obeying his Word.

But the starting point for everything Christian has to be grace-based. Actually, utterly unconditional grace empowers me to change. "Do not use your freedom to indulge the sinful nature," Paul writes in Galatians 5:13. Jesus plus nothing changes everything, while ironically, grace plus something drags me away from Jesus into a quagmire of human effort, frustration, and guilt (see Gal 5:1-4).

The stories are countless of people giving up on the church because they just couldn't bear the burden of unachievable religious demands. Paul had this in mind when he wrote, "Once I was alive apart from law; but when the commandment came, sin sprang to life and I died" (Rom 7:9). Rules put us back under the power of the law, performance orientation, the curse of the curve—and death. Grace always empowers us to change. That's the glorious good news. It's the gospel.

The apostles settled the matter forever in Jerusalem, in the first church conference ever: "Now then, why do you try to test God by putting on the necks of the disciples a yoke that neither we nor our fathers have been able to bear? No! We believe it is through the grace of our Lord Jesus that we are saved, just as they are" (Acts 15:10-11).

> My hope is built on nothing less
> Than Jesus' blood and righteousness.
> I dare not trust the sweetest frame,
> But wholly lean on Jesus' name.
> On Christ the Solid Rock I stand.
> All other ground is sinking sand.

God of Grace and Glory: Your unconditional and relentless love amazes me. How can I begin to fathom the boundless depths of such grace? Just for today, show me how to live out that liberty in a way that brings glory and honor to your name and gives others a fresh vision of the abundance of your grace. Amen.

....

FOUR

Misbelief 4:

God Is Love, So He'll Overlook What I'm Doing

Let us be thankful, and so worship God acceptably with reverence and awe, for our "God is a consuming fire."

HEBREWS 12:28

*T*wo Christian singles on the phone one Thursday evening....

"So, Amy, going skiing with Todd this weekend?"

"Don't know, Carrie. It's only been three months since my divorce was final. I don't think I'm ready for another relationship."

"Who said anything about a relationship? Take off after work Friday, hit the slopes Saturday, and drive back at a leisurely pace Sunday. Don't forget the hot tubs! Very romantic! You'll feel better in no time."

"What about church?"

"What about it? You can miss it once. God will understand that you need to relax."

If this scenario sounds farfetched to you, let me assure you it's not. According to recent surveys by Barna Research Group, when measuring the lifestyles, leisure habits, behaviors, and attitudes of born-again Christians and non-Christians, there is no appreciable difference, except that Christians go to church, give money to church, and have more Bibles in their homes. A startling 67 percent of those identified as born-again Christians said they did not believe in absolute truth.[1]

Christians just aren't what they used to be.

As a pastor of a large church, I am distressed over the shallowness and lack of moral convictions of so many believers, because I've watched people destroy themselves and their families in so many creative ways. Christians are much more in tune with the uncertain but compelling voices of our culture than they are with the unchanging standards of God's Word.

It's what I call godless Christianity. People profess to believe in Jesus, but they make decisions and live their lives as if God didn't exist. I mean, they're not terrible, evil people. They just hardly ever ask the question "What would Jesus do?"

Perhaps this is most evident in the premarriage counseling program at our church, where more than half of the couples who come to us for wedding services (some are older, but most are young) are already sexually active. Yes, Christians. Probably some Christians who are reading this book.

When we inform them that they cannot begin premarital counseling unless they agree to become sexually inactive until after their wedding, many couples argue with us. Some throw a fit. Others just smile and vanish. But we will not bend on this. I've told countless people, "I'm not a religious justice of the peace."

God has not called me to whitewash a serious violation of his law with a little smear of feel-good religion. I'm not in the business of doing weddings. I'm called to repair broken lives and build strong marriages and families. Living together while going through premarital counseling is like throwing dirt on your car as it comes out of the car wash. It's seriously counter-productive.

And everybody's *not* doing it.

People say things like "God understands. God is love. God isn't judgmental. Everyone sins in one way or another, and God is a compassionate, forgiving God. Who are we to judge?"

Bill Blather

"If any of you is without sin, let him be the first to throw a stone" (John 8:7). Did you hear that Bible quote a time or two when the nation was obsessed with President Clinton's personal problems?

As I'm writing this chapter, we're still trudging through that stinking mess, and just this last week I heard another round of talk-show babble. A female caller acknowledged confidently, "I voted for the president in the last election and, in a heartbeat, I would vote for him again."

"Why?" the host asked.

"Because," she replied, "if the government spent millions of dollars investigating my personal life, they'd find a whole lot more on me than they have on President Clinton."

The outrageously common logic: we're all sinners, and it

doesn't matter what you do in your private life as long as you're doing your job. This absurd opinion is held by two-thirds of the American public in most polls, and I'm convinced it's because their private lives are just as messy. "Live and let live" is everyone's motto. I won't judge you if you don't judge me.

And Now a Word From Our Sponsor

When people say that their private life is a private matter, what are they really saying? In many cases "privacy" is another word for "willful disregard." Disregard for the other person. Disregard for the truth. Most of all, disregard for God.

I am grieved by nit-picking, small-minded Christians, and deeply troubled about shallow Christians who think everything is black and white, who have simple answers for life's most difficult questions. But I'm *outraged* by "secular" Christians who have been fully immersed in the moral relativism of a post-Christian world. Their actions, in effect, deny the existence of God. Do they really think God doesn't know what's going on? Or, worse, that he doesn't care?

Jesus said, "You have heard that it was said, 'Do not commit adultery.' But I tell you that anyone who looks at a woman lustfully has already committed adultery with her in his heart" (Mt 5:27-28).

Am I missing something here? Doesn't the phrase "in his heart" have to do with every person's private life? The apostle Paul agreed with this principle when he wrote, "We have renounced secret and shameful ways; we do not use deception, nor do we distort the word of God. On the contrary, by setting forth the truth plainly we commend ourselves to every man's conscience in the sight of God" (2 Cor 4:2).

Tolerating a Stinking Mess?

Paul's diligent approach to embracing and disseminating truth is a far cry from the approach used by many Christians today:

"Live and let live."

"I won't judge you if you don't judge me."

"If any of you is without sin, let him be the first to throw a stone."

Many Christians confuse tolerance with forgiveness. But God doesn't tolerate sin. Yes, he forgives it, but in the New Testament "forgiveness" is an active, powerful word that means "to release."[2] When God forgives, he doesn't just look away from our bad side or tell himself, "Oh well, that's just the way they are." When God forgives, he releases us from the penalty and power of sin.

Maybe we could say God is a bit like a good dad whose darling baby's diaper is full of a stinking mess. Can't you hear all the nonjudgmentalists around us? "All babies stink! Deal with it! Love 'em anyway! Just look the other way and breathe through your mouth!"

I think what most parents do is change the dirty diaper and wash and powder the baby. Then, when the proper time comes, they teach the child to exercise self-restraint and refrain from making a stinking mess.

On Sins and Stones

The next time you hear someone quote John 8:7 (the stone-throwing verse) as an argument for tolerance, point out what happens in the original story. Some religious leaders dragged a woman into the public square. They had interrupted her in the act of sex, and her man wasn't her husband. (We have no idea what happened to him. Maybe he could just run faster.)

Can't you just imagine her quivering in humiliation and shame? And fear? According to Old Testament law, this woman was to be stoned to death. As they threw her to the ground in front of Jesus, can you detect the anguish in his eyes? You can almost see what he's thinking: *Stone her?! You want to stone her?!*

Perhaps softly, deliberately, he said, "If any one of you is without sin, let him be the first to throw a stone." And then he stooped down and began writing on the ground. "At this," John continues his narrative, "those who heard began to go away one at a time, the older ones first, until only Jesus was left, with the woman still standing there" (v. 9). Some people think Jesus was scribbling out the secret sins of all those sinners right there in the dirt.

Jesus straightened up and asked her, "Woman, where are they? Has no one condemned you?"

"No one, sir," she said.

"Then neither do I condemn you" (vv. 10-11).

Oh, for the story to end there. Oh, for a God of boundless love who overlooks our faults and indulges us in our sins.

But no.

"Go now and leave your life of sin," Jesus declared (v. 11). Change the stinking mess in your diaper.

Now, why would he say that? Was Jesus condemning the woman after all? Are we back to Jesus plus something? Absolutely not! But he knew full well the terrible consequences for anyone who persists in a life of sin, a life without the boundaries of God's Word.

"There is now no condemnation for those who are in Christ Jesus" (Rom 8:1), which means that we have been "justified," acquitted from the penalty of our sin. The ones who have their names written in the Lamb's Book of Life will not suffer the second death, the dreadful "lake of fire" (Rv 20:14-15). If you are in Christ and Christ is in you, God will not judge you in the *eternal* sense.

And it's true, God is not "judgmental" either. He's not short-tempered or mean-spirited. But that doesn't mean you can do whatever you want, that God is just so full of love that he can't help himself. God isn't that. Love without boundaries isn't love; it's dysfunctional infatuation. Real love has real boundaries.

The Bible says, "You have forgotten that word of encouragement that addresses you as sons: 'My son, do not make light of the Lord's discipline, and do not lose heart when he rebukes you, because the Lord disciplines those he loves, and he punishes everyone he accepts as a son.'

"Endure hardship as discipline; God is treating you as sons. For what son is not disciplined by his father? If you are not disciplined (and everyone undergoes discipline), then you are illegitimate children and not true sons" (Heb 12:5-8).

Slowly Sliding Into a Freezing Sea

Sometimes I feel downright desperate when I'm preaching. It's as if God's people are partying on the sloping decks of the *Titanic*, slowly sliding into a freezing sea. "For most of you," I've warned, "this is the only hour in your entire week that you're going to hear about the Christian worldview. Between now and next Sunday, a thousand voices on radio and television and on the job will assault what you're hearing this morning. For God's sake, don't let it happen!"

It's not that Christians don't know what the Bible says. It's just that they're drowning in a secular worldview that dominates the media, government, education, and workplace. Psalm 1 begins: "Blessed is the man who does not walk in the counsel of the wicked ["ungodly" in the King James] or stand in the way of sinners or sit in the seat of mockers." Notice the slide from walking to standing to sitting:

- *walking* along the road of godless advice;
- *standing*, coming to a position on something based on ungodly advice and participating in sinful behaviors;
- *sitting*, fully committed to the way the world thinks and mocking those who believe in truth or consequences.

The Counsel of the Ungodly

The "counsel of the ungodly" is any source of advice about life without reference to or regard for God. Godless people are not necessarily "bad" people, in the sense that they are perverted reprobates. It's just that God is a nonfactor for them.

"Secularism," a synonym of "godlessness," identifies a worldview that marginalizes God. Here's another way to say it:

- The Christian worldview: "In the beginning God…"
- The secular worldview: There is no beginning, and everything is random.

From the first four words of the Bible, we learn that everything starts with God. In stark contrast, the secular worldview is godless. It holds that God did not create human life purposefully in his image. Instead, human life is the result of random forces.

In the Beginning God…

Genesis 1:1 is the starting point of all biblical faith. It represents the basic difference between "traditional values" and what might be called "the new world order," which is really nothing more than a revival of the ancient paganism.

Primitive religions viewed the world as chaotic, disordered, random, accidental. But Hebrew religion saw the world as ordered. Everything had a place and purpose because all creation flows out of the heart of an all-wise God.

Creationism (which takes many forms) starts with God and believes that everything in the universe relates to God, who gives everything meaning, purpose, and connection. Genesis 1:1 is telling us that the world around us cannot be understood apart from the God who created it. Here's how this stuff works itself out.

The Unmoral Prophets

We are a godless, secular nation. A chilling article by best-selling Christian author Philip Yancey in a recent issue of *Christianity Today* magazine highlights our peril.

"The new science of evolutionary psychology attempts to explain all human thought and behavior as the unguided result of natural selection [random forces]. As products of blind evolution, say these thinkers [the 'unmoral prophets'], we deceive ourselves by searching for any teleology [meaning in life] other than that scripted in our DNA. We must look down, not up: to nature, not its Creator.

"News magazines like *Time* hire these writers to interpret gang behavior in the inner cities or sexual indiscretions in the capital city, and the results are so winsome that evolutionary psychologists have become the new cosmologists, helping us make sense of ourselves and our role in the universe."[3]

According to evolutionary psychology, I am driven by the need for my genetic material to perpetuate itself. Morality, then, springs entirely from my genes. What is right for my genes is right for me. "Carry the logic far enough, and any notion of good and evil disappears," writes Yancey. "Hardwired for selfishness, we have no potential for anything else."[4]

As evolutionary psychologist Richard Dawkins puts it, "We are survival machines—robot vehicles blindly programmed to preserve the selfish molecules known as genes. This is a truth which still fills me with astonishment. Though I have known it for years, I never seem to get fully used to it."[5]

As a Christian, I never *will* get used to it.

Inconsistent Moral Standards

Godless, secular people have no consistent moral standards, no clear understanding of what's right and what's wrong. Truth is relative, that is, it's all a matter of how you personally look at things. What's right for one person may not be right for somebody else.

"Without a God, you end up with a subjective morality. There's no way around that," said Rabbi Stewart Vogel in a recent interview. Coauthor with radio superstar Laura Schlessinger of their blockbuster book *The Ten Commandments: The Significance of God's Laws in Everyday Life,* Vogel added, "To believe in God is to believe that human beings are not mere accidents of nature. Without God, there is no objective meaning to life, and there is no objective morality. I don't want to live in a world where right and wrong are subjective."[6]

Declining Legal System

Human beings cannot live in a moral vacuum, so some form of law is necessary to maintain order in human society. Someone has to tell us what's right and what's wrong. And who's that going to be? A legal system, often constrained more by technicalities than the truth.

What better illustration than President Clinton in his videotaped testimony arguing, "It depends on what the meaning of 'is' is." What's more, much of the Kenneth Starr investigation of the president swirled around technical, court-determined definitions of sex.

Or did you hear about the "naked guy" incident at the University of California, Berkeley? James Dobson wrote about this one a couple years ago in his Focus on the Family newsletter. Administrators were paralyzed for months over what to do about the behavior of a student named Andrew Martinez, who made a practice of walking around the campus in the nude.

"He jogged, ate in the dining halls, and attended classes while totally naked," writes Dobson. "When asked why he wore no clothes, he said he was protesting sexually repressive traditions in Western society.... It is unbelievable that it took the Cal administrators all fall and winter to deal with this outrage. They couldn't come up with a legal excuse or a school regulation that would require 'the Naked Guy' to either suit up or ship out."[7]

Technicalities, not truth.

Anarchy Is Not Far Behind

If there are no moral standards, then ultimately I am not personally responsible to anyone else. I am responsible only to myself and to what I believe. An unusual admission in this regard appeared in, of all places, a *Time* magazine article, "The New Russia Culture: A Mind of Their Own." Correspondent John Kohan wrote, "When things go wrong in Russia, no one ever thinks that he personally might be to blame. *In contrast to Western Christianity*, the Russian Orthodox Church places little stress on the conception of personal guilt.... Russians routinely use the excuse that they are innocent victims of forces beyond their control to explain away personal failures" (italics mine).[8]

Russians routinely use that excuse? That they are "innocent victims of forces beyond their control"? Why does the author presume that Americans should be different? Because of the influence of Western Christianity? A secular writer is actually admitting that our spiritual roots determine what is right and what is wrong.

In a more recent article, written during Russia's 1998 economic crisis, a Russian commentator wrote for *Time,* "Most Russians have never realized that freedom requires responsibility, that it demands visceral, spiritual discipline.... This is Russia's historical mistake, and it goes back to Peter the Great. He admired Western factories and ships, but he never saw the spiritual and cultural traditions behind them."[9] Would he be referring to Judeo-Christian "cultural traditions"? Would that be the Bible he's talking about?

Stinkin' Thinkin'

An ancient Greek philosopher once wrote, "Bad beginnings always lead to bad endings." Perhaps it could be said that it's not how you finish but how you start. Start well, finish well.

"In the beginning God...." This is one of only two radically different worldviews, each of which has a radically different starting point and radically different applications and consequences.

The apostle Paul put it this way: "I tell you this, and insist on it in the Lord, that you must no longer live as the Gentiles do, in the futility of their thinking. They are darkened in their understanding and separated from the life of God because of the ignorance that is in them due to the hardening of their hearts" (Eph 4:17-18).

Below is a just a small sampling of "the futility of their thinking," popular godless myths that are demonstrably false, not only because the Bible says so, but because scientific research says so.

Myth: People need to be liberated sexually. The more liberated you are, the more fulfilled you will be in your sex life.

Fact: According to a recent study, the more traditional a person's view of sex, the more satisfied that person was in his or her sex life. Conversely, the less traditional (the less prudish?) the view of sex, the less satisfied a person was in his or her sex life.[10]

Fact: The stronger a married woman's religious beliefs, the more she is likely to feel satisfied with her sex life.[11]

Fact: According to a personal friend, the former chief gynecologist at Desert Samaritan Medical Center in Mesa, Arizona, recent clinical studies reveal that the more sexual partners a woman has, the greater the likelihood of her contracting cervical cancer.

Myth: If people get a divorce, it'll be better for the children because they won't hear all the fighting anymore. Children are resilient.

Fact: Research has demonstrated that children of divorce are far more likely to have serious social and educational problems.[12]

Myth: According to the Kinsey report, one in ten people is gay or lesbian.

Fact: Recent research findings reveal that the number is closer to one in one hundred, and monogamous relationships among gay males, persistently upheld as proof that the gay lifestyle is simply an alternative living arrangement, are statistically nonexistent.[13]

Myth: Religious people are dysfunctional.

Fact: Psychiatrist and medical researcher David Larson examined the data surrounding religion and good health during his ten years at the National Institute of Health. In 1992 he published a report in the *American Journal of Psychiatry* summarizing twelve years of psychiatric literature. He found that when measuring religious commitment (having a relationship with God and participating in religious services), more than 90 percent of the studies supported the view that religion benefits mental health.[14]

Fact: The lead article in a 1996 issue of the *American Psychological Association Monitor* reported that religious faith enhances mental health.[15]

Fact: In a recent survey of 1,473 people, Purdue University sociologist Kenneth Farraro found that practicing religion enhances your health.

Myth: You should live together before you get married in order to see if it's going to work out.

Fact: In a recent issue of *New Woman,* a feminist publication, Dr. Joyce Brothers published a potent list of reasons why couples should not cohabitate before marriage, including alarmingly higher incidents of divorce, sexual disease, and physical abuse of women.[16]

Myth: You will be happy if you have a successful career and lots of nice things.

Fact: "Whoever would love life and see good days must keep his tongue from evil and his lips from deceitful speech. He must turn from evil and do good; he must seek peace and pursue it" (1 Pt 3:10-11).

Guess Who's Knocking at Your Door?

In case you were wondering how I felt about all this, well, the Bible is more than a book of virtues—it's God's Word! And if you ignore it or disobey it, there will be terrible consequences.

"Do not be deceived," Paul wrote: "God cannot be mocked. A man reaps what he sows. The one who sows to please his sinful nature, from that sinful nature will reap destruction" (Gal 6:7-8). And this dreadful warning is from Galatians, which, as we saw in the last chapter, is Paul's most comprehensive and passionate defense of salvation by grace alone in the New Testament!

"Saved by grace" means that there is nothing I can do to earn my salvation. It's a gift of God, and Jesus is the author and finisher of my faith (see Eph 2:8; Heb 12:2). But "saved by grace" doesn't mean I'm saved from the temporal consequences of my sin.

I must confess, I've been hard-pressed at times to reconcile this with my grace-based approach to ministry, so I've thought this through to the following conclusions:

1. The Consequences of Sin Are Not Always Seen Right Away

If you sleep around or do drugs or just lie a little or whatever, God isn't immediately going to strike you dead with a bolt of lightning. You'll do something sinful and find that, well, nothing happened! No one found out. You didn't get pregnant or immediately contract some gruesome disease.

In fact, you think to yourself, *Man, that was so easy! Maybe it really doesn't matter what you do.* The Bible refers to this as "the pleasures of sin for a short time" (Heb 11:25). But it doesn't end there.

2. God Forgives Every Sin, But He Doesn't Overlook a Single One

When a remorseful criminal becomes deeply and genuinely religious and appeals for leniency, the judge may or may not let him off. In many cases, he won't.

Your relationship with God guarantees you a place in heaven *and* a good dose of heaven on earth no matter what you do, but it doesn't guarantee that you'll get out of jail if you've killed somebody, or that all the consequences of all your self-destructive behaviors will magically go away.

It's like getting a new car. You don't *have to* change the oil. You can drain it dry and drive it like the devil. No law against that! Do whatever you please, but if you don't follow the owner's manual, there will be a terrible price to pay. The Bible is your owner's manual. If you disregard its instructions, there will be consequences. It's inevitable.

3. The More You Do What You Shouldn't, the Easier It Becomes to Do Again (and the More You Risk)

The Letter of James says it this way, "Each one is tempted when, by his own evil desire, he is dragged away and enticed."[17]

We're all just human, and our humanity is enveloped by passions and filled with desires. God made us that way. But will you let your desires get the best of you? James explains, "After desire has conceived [when your passion has intercourse with your will], it gives birth to sin." Maybe just one sin. A manageable sin. Not so bad yet. But sin, James continues, "when it is full grown [sinning over and over, habit patterns], gives birth to death" (Jas 1:13-15).

A little sin here and a little bigger sin there, well, maybe nothing will happen. But persistent sin is terminal.

4. No Matter What You Do, God Isn't Going to Throw You out of the Family

Regardless of how frustrated I get with the mindless things I see Christians do, I won't cheapen the ministry, pervert the gospel,[18] or misrepresent God by scaring Christians into doing God's will for fear of hell. Jesus has delivered us once and for all and forever from the eternal penalty for sin. But I won't hesitate to tell Christians that, if they don't take God's Word seriously, they'll make a hell of their own lives and drag others through the fire with them.

Who wants that?

Listen to what happened to the Israelites and their families: "As for your children," God said, "that you said would be taken as plunder, I will bring them in to enjoy the land you have rejected. But you—your bodies will fall in this desert. Your children will be shepherds here for forty years, suffering for your unfaithfulness, until the last of your bodies lies in the desert" (Num 14:31-33).

They were God's children forever, those Hebrews. But their wayward lives kept them out of the Promised Land. God even took care of them in the desert, but they died there. And for forty years their children wandered with them in the wilderness of their self-destructive behaviors.

What people do to themselves and to the ones they love boggles my mind. A friend from Australia told me his family's sad story. His brother, a Christian man, ended his marriage and, simultaneously, his relationship with his children—all for the wild love of another woman. Years later, when his brother confessed inconsolable remorse for what he had done, my friend Ray asked him, "Didn't you count the cost?"

"Ray," his brother replied, "I counted the cost, but I greatly underestimated the consequences."

That reminds me of a story told by Frank Koch:

"Two battleships assigned to the training squadron had been at sea on maneuvers in heavy weather for several days. I was serving on the lead battleship and was on watch on the bridge as night fell. The visibility was poor with patchy fog, so the captain remained on the bridge keeping an eye on all activities.

"Shortly after dark, the lookout on the wing of the bridge reported, 'Light, bearing on the starboard bow.'

"'Is it steady or moving astern?' the captain called out.

"Lookout replied, 'Steady, Captain,' which meant we were on a collision course with that ship.

"The captain then called to the signalman, 'Signal that ship: "We are on a collision course, advise you to change course 20 degrees."'

"Back came the signal, 'Advisable for you to change course 20 degrees.'

"The captain said, 'Send, "I'm a captain. Change course 20 degrees."'

"'I'm a seaman second class,' came the reply. 'You had better change course 20 degrees.'

"By that time, the captain was furious. He spat out, 'Send, "I'm a battleship. Change course 20 degrees."'

"Back came the flashing light, 'I'm a lighthouse.'

"We changed course."[19]

There is a way that seems right to a man,
but in the end it leads to death.

PROVERBS 14:12

God of All Knowing: Search me, O God. What do you see in me that gives you grief? Tune my heart to hear that small voice of your Spirit. Not just because sin hurts me, but because it breaks your heart. Not because you don't love me as I am, but because you love me too much for me to stay this way. Amen.

....

Misbelief 5:

God Wants Me to Be Happy; He Will Always Protect Me From Pain and Suffering

Three times I pleaded with the Lord to take [my problem] away from me. But he said, "My grace is sufficient for you, for my power is made perfect in weakness."

2 CORINTHIANS 12:8-9

"Doesn't the Bible say that God wants me happy?" he asked sincerely.

I hardly knew what to say. Me. The author of many books. The guy with a thousand opinions. Me. Speechless.

You see, this wasn't a slice of an ordinary conversation. The man who asked me the question had been married for twenty-five years and wanted out. I had counseled with him and his wife at least half a dozen times, and I thought we were making progress. Then for months I heard nothing from them, until one day, I saw him in a restaurant sitting close to another woman.

Within a few weeks they were on my appointment calendar to ask if I would honor them by doing their wedding ceremony. Get this: not only had this man divorced his wife, but the woman he brought with him to my office was his wife's sister.

"I-I-I d-don't know what to say. I'm going to have to pray about this," I stuttered. "But, you know, it's going to be very difficult for me to give you my blessing."

"Well, fine," he retorted angrily. "We kind of expected that you wouldn't do our wedding, so we've already talked to another pastor about doing it for us, and he said he would if you didn't."

I gulped, "O-OK, fine."

I never saw them again.

And they lived happily ever after, right?

I bet not. And even if they did, I know for a fact that lots of people close to them, family and friends, were not "happy" about their decision. Some of them, such as his former wife, were enraged.

Life, Liberty, and the Pursuit of Happiness

I just got off the phone with a dear friend in our church. His wife has cancer. Actually, she's had massive treatments for cancer five times over the last fifteen years, but this time it's really grim. Her husband was calling for my support to mobilize a couple hundred people to pray around the clock for her healing. A miracle from God is her only hope.

I'd be surprised if, during this ordeal, my friend hasn't thought about his marriage vows a time or two: "for better, for worse; for richer, for poorer; in sickness and in health."

It's what pastors get young couples to say to one another,

because all of us older folks (I'll be fifty by the time this book is in your hands) know that life at its best is difficult, that "happily ever after" is a terrible myth.

But this is very difficult for Christians to understand, especially Christians in America, where our inalienable right and national obsession is "the pursuit of happiness." The search for happiness is so much a part of our national psyche that we just can't imagine why our personal well-being isn't God's personal priority.

"Happiness" means something very different to us today than it did to our Founding Fathers. Many people today believe they must protect their right to pursue, unfettered and at any cost, their own happiness.

Unfortunately, we have extended this idea to include God as well. Good American Christians have transformed the holy, wholly other God of the Bible into the maker of their personal success and the guarantor of their personal happiness. We will sacrifice our most cherished and important relationships, leave our church communities, even disobey God himself, all in the relentless pursuit of the elusive god of personal happiness.

Marriage has really taken a hit from the cult of happiness. Listen to what prominent, secular social scientists are saying, for example, about how the demand for happiness figures into the marriage and family crisis in America.

Marriage in America: A Report to the Nation, prepared by the politically diverse Council on Families in America, states boldly: "America's divorce revolution has failed.... Marriage has been losing its social purpose. Instead of serving as our primary institutional expression of commitment and obligation to others, especially children, marriage has increasingly been reduced to a vehicle—and a fragile one at that—for the emotional fulfillment of adult partners. 'Til death do us part' has been replaced by 'as long as I am happy.'"[1]

A God I Can Manage

In his masterpiece, *The Trivialization of God: The Dangerous Illusion of a Manageable Deity*, Donald McCullough coined the term "God of My Comfort," citing Robert Wuthnow, Princeton sociologist, who wrote, "At one time theologians argued that the chief purpose of humankind was to glorify God. Now it would seem that the logic has been reversed.... Spirituality no longer is true or good because it meets absolute standards of truth or goodness, but because it helps me get along. I am the judge of its worth.

"If it helps me find a vacant parking place, I know my spirituality is on the right track. If it leads me into the wilderness [figuratively speaking], calling me to face dangers I would rather not deal with at all, then it is a form of spirituality I am unlikely to choose."[2]

Donald McCullough also decries what he calls the "God of My Success." "Success," he writes, "isn't what it's cracked up to be." A best-selling author, Dan Wakefield had his first novel, *Going All the Way*, published in 1970. McCullough reports that it was chosen as a top award winner of the Literary Guild, hit the *Time* magazine best-seller list for three weeks, and sold more than eight hundred thousand copies in paperback.

Wakefield said of his personal success, "The dream of a lifetime had been realized, and I was delighted. I was also nervous and anxious.... Success and achievement and rewards are all fine, but they do not transform you, do not bring about a state of built-in contentment or inner peace or security, much less salvation.... [My first] novel was not The Answer to all of life's problems. I had another drink."[3]

But what if you're successful for God? The demons of low self-esteem and depression have been my constant companions, and they've been in my family for generations. Depression, simplistically defined, is the absence of happiness from a sense of failure or loss. So to compensate for my feelings of personal emptiness and pain, I've also always been a high achiever. I've "made it big" in the ministry, which should be the most rewarding career on God's earth. Our church has more than six thousand members, a brand-new two-thousand-seat worship center, and this is my sixth book.

Should I be happy? Oh yes, I am profoundly grateful to God for the extraordinary ways he has used me, but sorry, I still get depressed. I've had to acknowledge over and over that bad things don't make me depressed, and success doesn't make my depression go away. Like Paul, I have had to learn how to be content whatever my circumstances, that I can do all things through Christ who strengthens me.

So, What Do You Think Is Going to Make You Happy?

Let's start with a definition: Happiness is the sense of well-being a person gets from his or her circumstances, including four basic elements of life: reasonably good health, a good family and friends, a job that promotes a sense of purpose and value, and a modest accumulation of nice things.

Not too much to ask, do you think? Would *you* be happy if you pretty much had those four things? Would you still be happy if, say, you had only two or three of the elements, like good health and a decent job, but you also had old, beat-up cars and furniture and a dysfunctional family?

Or would you still be happy if you had all four elements, including generally good health, except for severe allergies six months of the year? Not life-threatening, just a lot of sneezing, itchy eyes, and stuffy nose. Would you be happy?

Or, let's say, you had all four elements, including a wonderful family of five: you, your spouse, and your three children. Except one of your children is in a wheelchair. Or one of your children is barely making it through high school. Or one of your children has just one eye. Would you be happy?

Circumstantial Happiness?

Happiness based on circumstances, any circumstances, is utterly elusive. *Circumstance* is a word that means "stand around." *Happiness*, of course, comes from the same English root from which we get the word "happens." Happiness based on circumstances is however you feel about whatever happens around you. Happiness based on circumstances or possessions or personal achievements is a black hole.

Circumstances aren't ever going to make you happy.

I am grateful whenever anything goes my way. My daughter

just got engaged, and both families think they're wonderful for each other. I just returned from a great, relatively stress-free family vacation. At this moment I'm working on this book in one of the most lovely settings in Arizona: the Verde River Valley near the world-famous red rocks of Sedona. It's a gorgeous day. Our church had a good offering last Sunday. I'm grateful for a lot of things, but things change, and they can change suddenly, traumatically. What then?

What may come as a shock to a great number of Christians is that the Bible is relatively silent on the subject of happiness. The word "happiness" doesn't appear even once in the *King James Version*, and "happy" pops up only about two dozen times, mostly in Psalms and Proverbs where the Hebrew word means "greatly blessed."

The Greek equivalent in the New Testament, *makarios* (which also means "greatly blessed"), is seldom translated by the English word "happy." One place this word appears is near the end of Jesus' lengthy final instructions to his disciples in the Upper Room the night of his arrest: "If ye know these things, happy are ye if you do them" (John 13:17, KJV). The *New International Version* translates this, "you will be blessed." According to Jesus, true happiness is obeying God!

Jesus used a form of the same Greek word, *makarios*, at the beginning of each of the eight Beatitudes in Matthew 5:3-10:

- "Blessed [happy] are the poor in spirit."
- "Blessed [happy] are those who mourn."
- "Blessed [happy] are the meek."
- "Blessed [happy] are those who hunger and thirst for righteousness."

- "Blessed [happy] are the merciful."
- "Blessed [happy] are the pure in heart."
- "Blessed [happy] are the peacemakers."
- "Blessed [happy] are those who are persecuted."

Why, I think we just stumbled onto the definition of true happiness. I take it all back! The Bible *does* say that God wants me to be happy, and Jesus tells me how to get there. Clearly, it's not on the great American road in a new BMW roadster (something I've dreamed of owning. That'll make me happy for sure!).

The idea that happiness is a sense of well-being based on circumstances is simply not in the Bible. In fact, the biblical authors could not have conceived of a God whose purpose was to rearrange their circumstances in order to make their lives easier. Two thousand years ago ordinary life was indescribably difficult. If you want to sample what it was like at the time of Jesus, visit a developing nation like Malaysia or Mexico.

And for Christians, it was even worse.

Back then, if you decided to become a believer, you put your life on the line. Becoming a Christian was not a highway to a better, more fulfilling, happier life. Instead, it meant your life might be cut short. In the early church bad things happened to good people all the time, and few tried to figure out why a good God would do that to them. They were just grateful that God gave them extraordinary grace whenever they needed it.

The early Christians never believed that God was on their side just to make life easier or more comfortable. God was there for them to make a very difficult life more tolerable. God was present, not to get them out of their personal problems, but to sustain them through whatever came their way.

This is precisely Paul's perspective on God and tough times: "No temptation has seized you except what is common to man. And God is faithful; he will not let you be tempted beyond what you can bear. But when you are tempted, he will also provide a way out so that you can stand up under it" (1 Cor 10:13).

Did you catch that? God could make the temptation go away, but he doesn't. Instead, he gives us the strength to "stand up under it," to endure it, no matter how long it lasts. Paul, of course, was speaking from personal experience: "Three times I pleaded with the Lord to take it [apparently a health problem] away from me. But he said, 'My grace is sufficient for you, for my power is made perfect in weakness'" (2 Cor 12:8-9).

For the first Christians, God was not only their source of every blessing but also their strength in every loss. God was there on both ends of life. "They called the apostles in and had them flogged.... The apostles left ... rejoicing [happy?] because they had been counted worthy of suffering disgrace for the Name" (Acts 5:40-41).

Happily Contented

Contentment brings happiness, inner joy, and peace. Not the other way around. "Godliness with contentment," Paul wrote to Timothy, "is great gain" (1 Tim 6:6). Paul didn't write, "Godliness with great gain is contentment."

Probably the best piece of literature ever on the theme of

contentment is Paul's Letter to the Philippians, in which he wrote that he had "learned to be content whatever the circumstances. I know what it is," he said, "to be in need, and I know what it is to have plenty" (Phil 4:11-12). In other words, when I have it bad, I don't get too low, and when I have it good, I don't get too high, because I know that everything in this life, bad and good, is temporary.

"I have learned to be content," *learned* it, because being content is not in the gene pool. The day you're born, you scream about your discontentment. And you'll scream many more times before you learn to be content. And even after you do, you'll still probably scream from time to time.

"I have learned to be content in any and every situation," Paul wrote, "whether well fed or hungry, whether living in plenty or in want," whether living out the American dream or living in a cardboard shack in Tijuana with the American dream just a ditch and a chain-link fence away. "I can do everything," Paul concludes, "through Christ who gives me strength" (v. 13). God won't give me everything I want, but I can make it with whatever I have, because Jesus is in me to give me strength.

The Freedom of Letting Go

The way I can learn to be content is through the most excellent freedom of letting go. Anxiety, the opposite of contentment, has a lot to do with loss of control. When I hang my happiness on things I can't control, and those things change, I lose my peace.

Listen carefully to one of Jesus' best-loved promises: "Come to me, all you who are weary and burdened, and I will give you rest. Take my yoke upon you and learn from me, for I am gentle and humble in heart, and you will find rest for your souls. For my yoke is easy and my burden is light" (Mt 11:28-30).

What, specifically, is Jesus talking about? What's he offering us? Personal peacefulness? A sense of well-being? Happiness? Actually, all of those things and none of those things. Look at the passage again carefully. Jesus' promise is specific: rest for our souls. Does this mean anything to you? Are you leaping into the depths of this, or does it just sound soothing?

Every Jewish listener, every reader of the Gospel of Matthew, which was written mostly for Jewish readers, would pick up immediately on the underlying meaning of this promise. They would know that Jesus wasn't speaking therapeutically: "Come to me for treatment, and I'll help you clear your head." No. Jesus was, in effect, announcing that he was the Messiah, the one who would fulfill the rich symbolism of the ancient Jewish Sabbath, the day of rest.

Weekly, the Israelites were to remember that God was in control of everything and they were in control of nothing. Making a ritual of true happiness, the Sabbath was a celebration of the most excellent freedom of letting go.

The Pause That Refreshes

Remember the old Coke advertising slogan? "It's the pause that refreshes." You can still see it on vintage pop machines and faded tin signs along the old two-lane highways of America. The Hebrew word for Sabbath comes from a root term that means "to cease, to pause." The Sabbath was a weekly, twenty-four-hour "pause" to rest and refresh your memory about you and God.

God made everything, and on the seventh day, he paused and said, "Mmm, this is good." The Sabbath remembers that God made it all (see Ex 31:17), and what God made, God owns. So give it up. Take a break from trying to run your own life. Pause and turn it all back to God.

The Sabbath was always supposed to point to God, be about God—like salvation, like all of life. By the time of Christ, however, the day of freedom had evolved into a day of enslavement to rigid rules. The focus had shifted from God's good, finished work to man's feeble, petty works. Scripture tells us that Jesus was strongly criticized by the religious elite of his day for healing the sick on the Sabbath, because technically that was work (see Lk 6:1-11).

Overly pious people had perverted God's reason for The Pause, which was to be a sign of grace. Every week God wanted to remind his people that they couldn't be holy enough to save their own souls: "You must observe my Sabbaths," God said. "This will be a sign between me and you for the generations to come, so you may know that *I am the Lord, who makes you holy"* (Ex 31:12, italics added).

A prophetic image, the Sabbath also pointed to the future when the Messiah would bring peace to the whole earth: "In that day the Root of Jesse will stand as a banner for the peoples; the nations will rally to him, and *his place of rest* will be glorious"

(Is 11:10, italics added). This is what people heard in their hearts when Jesus announced, "Come to me, all you who are weary and burdened, and I will give you rest." This was the long-awaited Messiah talking to them!

Creation and the Cross

When God created the universe in six days, he did it all. He did it perfectly. There was absolutely nothing more to do, nothing that you or I could add to it.

Dying on the cross, Jesus shouted, "It is finished!" He did it all. He did it perfectly. There was absolutely nothing more to do. You can enjoy salvation, you can live and rest in Christ's finished work, but you can't add a thing to it. If you do, it's a knock on Jesus.

For us to presume that we have to do more to earn our salvation, to add something to what Jesus has already done, is to imply that what Jesus accomplished at Calvary was not quite enough. It would be like working on the Sabbath. Paul had this in mind when he declared, "I do not set aside the grace of God, for if righteousness could be gained through the law, Christ died for nothing!" (Gal 2:21).

R.I.P.

Our teenage son, Matt, is extraordinarily conscientious. At the sound of his alarm, he gets himself up every morning at 5:30 to take care of his pets and get ready for school, which for him starts before 7:00 A.M. with marching band practice. But give him a Saturday or summer vacation, and he's still in a coma well past noon.

As hard as Matt works in school, the truth of the matter is that he totally depends on me—on my love, my support, and my money.

I work. Matt sleeps.

Jesus finished the work. I rest.

The Letter to the Hebrews, which unwraps many of the Old Testament symbols, ties this all together: "There remains, then, a Sabbath-rest for the people of God; for anyone who enters God's rest also rests from his own work, just as God did from his" (Heb 4:9-10).

Entering into rest is, essentially, learning how to be content. Pausing to rest one day a week, the Israelites remembered that they were wholly dependent on God for everything, which brings us full circle: "I have learned," Paul boasted, "the secret of being content [the secret of The Pause to release everything back to God] in any and every situation, whether well fed or hungry, whether living in plenty or in want. I can do everything through him who gives me strength" (Phil 4:12-13).

Three Men and Their Babies

I was in Colombia last spring—against the best advice of the U.S. State Department, which urged American citizens to stay out of there, especially the city of Cali. Well, after a lot of prayer and consultation, I went there anyway. While in the former capital of the narcotrade, I met Ruth Ruibal, whose husband, Julio, a leading pastor in that city of nearly two million, had been shot to death in front of a church.

With the highest per capita murder rate in the world, there is no place more dangerous than Colombia. Three American missionaries vanished there several years ago, and their families still don't know if they're dead or alive. Recent information suggests they are no longer living.

Ever had one of your kids, or perhaps your spouse, come home hours after you expected him or her? Missing children posters—they caught my eye at Wal-Mart earlier today—give me the chills. I really have no personal experience in this, but it seems like the disappearance of someone you love would be more traumatic to go through than their death. It must be so, because families are often "relieved" when a body is finally recovered after a long, mysterious absence.

How are the wives of those three missionaries coping? Do you think they have any reason to be "happy"? Is it possible for someone in their plight actually to find contentment and rest in Christ the way Paul describes it in Philippians 4?

You decide. I'll let the wives of Mark, David, and Rick speak for themselves.

"Those guerrillas have taken everything away from our husbands and lots away from us and our children, but one thing they can't take away from us is our right to choose joy no matter what happens in our lives" (Tania Rich, wife of hostage Mark Rich).

"It's a trial of our faith. Since this happened, I have read Scripture with a new light, and my faith has grown deeper. I have realized that God doesn't tell us he'll get us out of situations, but he'll be our strength through them" (Nancy Mankins, wife of hostage David Mankins).

"We make a choice every day to pry our hands loose and give our husbands up to the Lord, saying, 'They're yours, Lord. Dave, Mark, and Rick are yours. Our lives are yours, and you can do whatever you please with them.' That's not easy, but every time I do, God is there to catch me up and help me walk above the circumstances" (Patti Tenenoff, wife of hostage Rick Tenenoff).[4]

In this chapter I've said just about everything I can about happiness and contentment. These three women have said it all.

....

God of the Sabbath: Thank you, not only for giving me the strength to get through the circumstances of life, but also for giving me the grace to be content no matter what happens. May I remember every day to look past the highs and lows of daily living to you, the source of true happiness. Amen.

....

....

SIX

Misbelief 6:

If God Leads Me to Do Something, Everything Will Always Work Out Great

This man is my chosen instrument to carry my name before the Gentiles and their kings and before the people of Israel. I will show him how much he must suffer for my name.

ACTS 9:15-16

Y ou never know where the road of life is going to take you.

Mark and Kristina didn't have it easy, but generally life was pretty good. Both of them had met Christ in the San Francisco Bay area in 1970, and Mark, a gifted communicator with a heart for God, wound up in full-time Christian ministry.

Within a few more years, Mark was serving as the presiding pastor of a small network of churches in Marin County, north of the Bay. Their heartache was Matt, the oldest of their four children, who had severe asthma. The damp air of the northern California coast was making him worse.

Doctors told Matt's parents they had to move to a drier climate, like Arizona's. So after serious prayer with the other leaders of their ministry network, Mark and Kristina decided to relocate to Phoenix. Never ones to back away from an adventure, they decided the move was an opportunity. They believed it was God's will for them to plant a church in their new city. And so Mark and Kristina followed the example of Abraham, who "obeyed and went, even though he did not know where he was going" (Heb 11:8).

God was leading Mark and Kristina, and just about everything was working out great. After a couple of years of faithful ministry, their new church started growing rapidly and Mark launched a popular Christian radio talk show, hosted programs on the local Christian television station, and began writing a monthly article for a national Christian magazine for pastors.

Things were good, and then—*wham!*—out of nowhere came every mom and dad's worst nightmare. Recovering nicely from the asthma, Matt left for a day trip to the Salt River outside of Phoenix. He never came home. The faithful couple's sixteen-year-old son—one of the finest young men you'd ever hope to meet—went to be with Jesus in a drowning accident. It hurts to write this, because his father, Mark, is one of my best friends.

Why did God let that happen? How could he lead Mark and Kristina to Phoenix for the health of their son, only to stand back and let Matt die? Maybe God didn't lead them to Phoenix in the first place. If they knew then what they know now, maybe they never would have left California.

Or worst of all thoughts, maybe there was something wrong with them. Maybe they didn't have enough faith. Maybe God was angry about something.

Unraveling the Tangle of Bad Decisions

You never know where the road of life is going to take you. The assumption of most Christians is that, if you have a clear sense that God is leading you to do something, everything will work out just great. If it doesn't, the decision must not have been from God.

Take marriage.

Are you married? Did you think it was God's will at the time? If it was God's will, and you think everything works out great in God's will, then why did you promise to stay together "for better or for worse; for richer or for poorer; in sickness and in health"? Did you assume that everything might *not* work out just great? Not that you expected the worst, but were you at least realistic enough to know that marriage would be a lifelong learning experience? Many weddings now leave the "for better or for worse" stuff out because some young couples think it's a negative confession. I feel very negative about that.

Well, if marriage is not a problem for you, how about that new job? Did you pray about that one? Did you have a sense that God was guiding you when you accepted the offer?

Or the school you decided to attend?

Or the house you decided to buy?

Or the kids you decided to have? Have you had any surprises raising those kids?

Or do you feel that your life is a miserable tangle of bad decisions and meaningless events? Are you sinking in the quicksand of your past? Are you confused? If you've had trouble finding God in the mess you've made of your life (or maybe you feel you're an entirely innocent victim), let me help.

You never know where the road of life is going to take you, and just because you have a sense that God is leading you does not mean that everything is going to work out just great. But, as I'm going to show you in this chapter, wherever the road of life takes you, God will be there to meet you.

Ask Mark and Kristina. They'd be the first to tell you that the bright light of God beamed into their darkest night.

This whole problem—expecting things to work out just great, and then being very disappointed, even disillusioned when they don't—is a twist on the theme of the last chapter. Remember? The relentless pursuit of happiness? It's what we unwittingly allow to affect the way we pray and what we expect of God.

Instead of looking to do the *right* thing, we pester God to lead us to the *best* thing. Asking for God's will becomes a search for the option that will bring us the greatest success with the least effort. So we wait on God to discover his "perfect" will, because if we're not in his "perfect" will, something bad might happen.

Here's how this works. We know that God knows the future (if you're not sure of that, reread chapter 1). So because he knows what lies ahead, we expect God to lead us away from the worst job to the best one. From the worst neighbors to the best ones. From singleness to the best possible marriage.

What's more, we have the mistaken idea that the will of God is some place or position or job. Yes, God cares deeply about where we go, where we live, and every little thing we do, but he cares mostly about *how* we live regardless of *where* we live, how we apply ourselves to *whatever* job he gives us, and how we learn to love the one we marry.

It's the same old same old: "Whatever my circumstances," Paul wrote, "I have learned to be content. I can do all things, work just about any job, love my spouse and my kids, support my local church, get along with my neighbors, through Christ who strengthens me" (see Phil 4:12-13).

Yes, I can.

Yes, you can.

Michael Jordan on Faith

Our compulsive, obsessive need for happiness, for everything to work out just great, prevents us from learning from God when things don't work out so great. So we end up spending a huge amount of mental and emotional energy mulling over the would've, could've, should've. And because it keeps us stuck in the past, we can't seem to do anything with our future. Fearful of making the wrong decision, one that might be out of the will of God (which means we would really be unhappy), we stand paralyzed at the crossroads of opportunity.

Nike has good basic advice for all of us apprehensive people: Just do it. Michael Jordan just does it. I'll never forget watching in amazement as he single-handedly won the sixth game of his final championship series against the Utah Jazz. Utah was ahead by three points with less than a minute left in the game. Not a problem for Michael, who made a quick basket, stole the ball from Utah's best player, Karl Malone, and made another quick basket. In what seemed like a miracle moment, the Bulls won championship number six—by one point.

Have you seen Michael Jordan's commercial about failure? I grabbed my sermon outline legal pad and took notes: "I've missed over nine thousand shots in my career. I've been given the ball in game-winning situations twenty-seven times, and missed the shot. I've failed over and over again. That's why I succeed."

Go for it!

Nothing Ventured, Nothing Gained

We owned our previous house for over ten years. So many memories. As we were getting ready to move, I cried as I sorted papers into boxes.

Moving was difficult for the previous owners of our new house, too. During the time they lived here, they had lost their oldest son, killed in a motorcycle accident just a few blocks away. A memorial tree for their David shades my study window. I can see it now, right outside, just a few feet from the desk where I'm working.

As we talked about the pain of change, the former owner of our home said something so simple, something I'll never forget. "We've taught our children," she said proudly, "make the best possible decision with the information available at the time, and don't look back."

Michael Jordan and the former owner of our home—they have the faith of Abraham, too. And as far as I know, they're not even what we would call "born-again Christians"! How can God's children be so tentative and fearful when the world is outrageously bold? Why is that? We're so concerned about doing the best thing that we don't do anything.

Here's a summary of the scenario of dumb, debilitating things that smart Christians believe about finding God's will for their lives:

- God's will for your life is completely predetermined.

- You will be happy when you find out exactly what that is and do it—and unhappy when you don't.

- God won't tell you what his will is, so life is a big guessing game with God as you try to determine his will for your life. (It's like you're playing Battleship with God: Hit! Miss. Hit! Hit! Miss. Miss. Miss.)

- You mustn't do anything or take any risks until you know exactly what God wants you to do, because you don't want to be out of God's will.

- When you make a bad decision, you'll know it because everything doesn't work out just great, which means for sure you weren't doing the will of God.

- Of course, you'll know you've made the right decision, and that you're right in the middle of God's perfect will, if everything is working out just great. And you're happy, of course.

Think about it: If faith is the evidence of things not seen (see Heb 11:1), are you really living by faith if you always know exactly what God wants you to do before you do it? Every decision in life is thorny with risks, and the greater the opportunity for success, the bigger the chance for failure.

Just ask your banker. The highest yields in the investment market always carry the highest risks. Put your money in a no-risk savings account, and inflation will outrun your interest.

Was It God, or Was It the Baklava?

In Acts 16 we read an account of the boldness of Paul in the face of extraordinary uncertainty. He knew what it meant to press forward even when he didn't know the precise will of God for his life.

"Paul and his companions," Luke reports, "traveled throughout the region of Phrygia and Galatia, having been kept by the Holy Spirit from preaching the word in the province of Asia. When they came to the border of Mysia, they tried to enter Bithynia, but the Spirit of Jesus would not allow them to. So they passed by Mysia and went down to Troas" (Acts 16:6-8).

Did you just blow by that passage, like everybody else who speed-reads these parts of the Bible to get to the more meaty, spiritual stuff? Well, if you did, you'll miss the whole point of the chapter. Paul, you see, was trying to find the will of God, and he didn't have a clue. Those two "insignificant" verses record *weeks* of walking—rather aimlessly—around Asia Minor, which is modern-day Turkey. Actually it was a thousand miles of walking! And all Paul could say was that God did not want him in Asia ("kept by the Holy Spirit from preaching") or Bithynia ("the Spirit of Jesus" didn't like that idea, either). No explanation from God. No other suggestions. Out of options and worn out from all the walking.

But Paul kept going, kept pressing forward, taking risks, still not knowing precisely God's will. Finally, "during the night Paul had a vision of a man from Macedonia standing and begging him, 'Come over to Macedonia and help us.' After Paul had seen the vision, we got ready at once to leave for Macedonia, concluding that God had called us to preach the gospel to them" (vv. 9-10).

Finally, a leading from God! How could anything go wrong? Well, God was leading, but a lot of things went wrong. After a few more weeks (we can't be sure from the text precisely how much time had elapsed), there's still no record of significant ministry, except an unusual event that came more out of Paul's personal frustration than any strategic ministry plan.

A young fortune-teller kept annoying Paul and his companions until, finally, "Paul became so troubled that he turned around and said to the spirit, 'In the name of Jesus Christ I command you to come out of her!' At that moment the spirit left her" (v. 18)—and all hell broke loose. Before they knew what was happening, Paul and Silas were dragged before the city officials, "severely flogged," and thrown brutally into the inner dungeon of the local prison (v. 23).

There they were. In chains. At midnight. And as Paul and Silas sat there aching in that dank, disgusting jail, they started "singing hymns to God" (v. 25).

This is what *didn't* happen, what *wasn't* said: "So, Paul," Silas whimpered, "could you run through that Macedonian vision once more? Was that God, or was that the second helping of baklava we had the night before? If I had known then, Paul, what I know now, I would never have made this trip with you. If God had led us here, everything should have worked out just great. I'm not so sure anymore about the leading of God in this. After all, why would such a good God let such a bad thing happen to two of the nicest people you could ever meet?"

No, none of that. Instead, they chanted new Christian songs, and as they sang, "the other prisoners were listening to them." People in that prison were about to be changed forever because of the godly response of Paul and Silas. Everything wasn't working out so great, but these two men were determined to make the best of it.

Suddenly there was a great earthquake, and Paul and Silas were delivered! But I don't want to go there. That's the part of the story Christians hear over and over. Instead, I want you to reflect on Paul and Silas' response to the terrible turn of events. You never know where the road of life is going to take you, but wherever you end up, God will be there to meet you.

In the end God worked everything together for good. The Philippian jailer and his entire family became Christians, and we know from Paul's later Letter to the Philippians that a solid and influential Christian community was formed in that city. But the lesson is clear: Just because God leads you to do something doesn't mean that everything is going to work out the way you want it to, that you are going to be happy.

Like Paul and Silas, though, you can sing hymns to God, you can praise your way through it, reminding yourself that all the hell in your life is not just about you, about your personal suffering, about you being a bad person. No! Like the prisoners a few iron doors down the corridor from Paul's cell, all the people in your life are listening to you. They're watching to see how you handle adversity, to see if Jesus is as real in your life as you say he is, or if you just praise him when he makes you happy.

Friends of Mark and Kristina were changed forever when we heard them sing beautiful hymns to God at midnight. They're still singing. Their son Matt is singing in heaven too. Can you hear them?

Great God of Heaven: Give me the faith to go wherever you guide me, no matter what the cost. I confess that I am sometimes discouraged from listening to the promptings of your Spirit when the path ahead looks too steep or rocky. Give me the courage to follow anyway. Amen.

....

Misbelief 7:

If I Pray Enough and Work on It, Someday My Problem Will Go Away

I've tried everything and nothing helps. I'm at the end of my rope. Is there no one who can do anything for me? Isn't that the real question?

ROMANS 7:24, THE MESSAGE

Overheard at a weight loss support group in a church far, far away....

"So, Ginny, how did your family reunion go?"

"Well ... it was tough, but I'm glad I went. My Aunt Maude came with her new husband and her specialty cheesecake. It was really hard on my Uncle Phil when they got divorced and she ran off with Richard. Somehow I managed to keep my mouth shut at the reunion."

"You didn't tell her off?"

"Of course I told her off. But I didn't eat the cheesecake!"

I have a problem. Actually, I have a lot of problems, but I'd like to tell you about one in particular: I have a short fuse. It's been like this as long as I can remember. My mother could tell you about it. My wife. My kids. People who have worked with me.

I mean, sometimes I just lose it, especially if I'm tired or under a lot of stress. I've said things I regret terribly, and I've embarrassed myself in public places.

I get angry about all the things people get angry about: Other drivers on the freeway. My lawnmower quitting with just two rows left to mow. Hanging curtain rods. The digging dogs. Differences between my wife and me. And, of course, people at church. Generally, I get angry when things don't go my way.

Now, I've never physically hurt anybody, never been arrested for getting into a brawl. My anger has never been as bad as it could be, but it's never been as controlled as it should be.

I've prayed about it. Fasted for freedom from it. Received counsel and prayer for it. Read books about it. Preached on it. And now I'm writing about it, but not to tell you how to overcome your anger problem in five simple steps.

I'm baring all to help you understand and accept the fact that who you are, in a certain sense, will never change. Does that blow you away? Does that statement make you angry? Please hear me out on this. In some ways it may be the most important and liberating thing I have to say in this whole book, but it's going to take a lot of explaining on my part and a lot of rethinking on yours.

May I say it again? Who you are, in a certain sense, will never change. I know, this seems to fly in the face of everything every pastor has said in every pulpit in Christian history, that if you love Jesus, if you pray, if you listen to sermons, if you have others pray for you, you will change. It's one of the reasons why God gave us the Bible, right?

I agree! As a pastor, I preach for change. I wrote this book on the premise that people will read it, change the way they think, and ultimately change their behaviors. Paul made this clear when he wrote one of his better-known passages, "Do not conform any longer to the pattern of this world, but be transformed by the renewing of your mind" (Rom 12:2).

Any Old Pot Will Do

Sanctification is the biblical and theological word for the process of change that occurs after we become Christians. The Greek term translated *sanctify* means, literally, "to make holy." But what does that mean? What does it mean to be "holy"? It's really pretty basic. The Bible concept of "holiness" means simply "to set apart." So, in one sense, to be sanctified doesn't mean that everything about you changes.

The pots and bowls used to serve in the ancient Jewish temple were regular, ordinary vessels. But when they were put in the temple, they became "sanctified." Same pot, new place and new purpose. Still looked like the same old pot, but it was dedicated to God.

It's not the pot that counts. It's what's in the pot! Remember the story of Jesus' first miracle, turning water into wine at the wedding feast at Cana? Those old stone jars were full of wash water—until they met Jesus! Then, suddenly, they were full of the finest wine (see Jn 2:1-11). Any old pot will do if it's set apart, "sanctified" for the Master's use.

Have You Been Set Apart?

When I become a Christian, God does not change my personality. He doesn't even try, because my personality is the way he made me. What does happen, though, is that God takes my imperfect pot and puts it under the lordship of Christ. He sanctifies it.

Take my anger, for example. A good, positive way for me to look at my anger is to see it as an expression of a deeply passionate personality. In the right time and place, under the lordship of Christ, God uses that side of me. When I preach, sometimes I sound angry. I can be excitable and exciting. "Wow, God was speaking to me in that sermon!" people tell me. Maybe that's why one of my favorite Scriptures is "Be ye angry, and sin not" (Eph 4:26, KJV).

So God isn't obsessed with making my anger go away. If he did that to me, something about my essential nature would change. Some people probably think I could use a lobotomy. It would really calm me down, and my struggle with my anger would go away forever. But then I would be a terrible preacher.

My personality, my gifts, *me*—when I'm under the lordship of Christ, sanctified and set apart for him, it's a beautiful thing! But when my personality, my gifts, *me*—when I'm my own master, I make my life and the lives of everyone around me thoroughly miserable.

When you become a Christian, you get to be you! So I'll repeat my main idea in this chapter: Who you are, in a certain sense, will never change. Do I have your attention?

What are *you* struggling with? What's always been just outside the circle of your complete control? What's so much a part of you that you just can't accept? That you just can't make go away?

- Insomnia?

- Depression?

- Lethargy?

- A messy home? Office?

- Your weight?

- Anxiety?

- Talking too much? Not talking enough?

- Too much television?

- "Stuck" in grief over a personal loss?

- Sexual addiction? Or "just" lustful thoughts?

Jesus said that if a man merely looks on a woman in the wrong kind of way, he has committed adultery in his heart and is guilty of breaking the seventh commandment. Would the men out there who have mastered this one please stand up? (Actually, I did counsel with a man one time who told me he's never tempted in his thoughts about women, but he's definitely attracted to good-looking men!)

And if sins of commission aren't your problem, what about sins of omission? Are you confident that you pray often enough, long enough, attentively enough? What have you been trying to overcome for the last five, ten, or forty years of your life? And how do you deal with your failure—and the shame associated with it?

Leaving the Shadowlands

I come to Christ "just as I am," but I can't stay that way; every Bible verse, every sermon, every song, reminds me that I should be different. Instead of lingering in the dark shadow of who I am, I'm always reminded to live in the blinding light of what I should be.

I'm so glad Paul wrestled with this same problem: "I find this law at work: when I want to do good, evil is right there with me. For in my inner being I delight in God's law; but I see another law at work in the members of my body, waging war against the law of my mind and making me a prisoner of the law of sin at work within my members. What a wretched man I am! Who will rescue me from this body of death?" (Rom 7:21-24).

The Christian community is (dare I say it?) obsessed with the task of changing people. It's not surprising, given everything the Bible says about becoming a new person in Christ. But tragically the Christian community is not always prepared, sometimes not willing, to accept people if they don't change or won't change.

The church is an environment that insists on radical change, often as a condition of acceptance and at the expense of grace that patiently allows change to occur. Physician and Christian counselor Dwight Carlson calls this the myth of the emotional health gospel, which "assumes that if you have repented of your sins, prayed correctly, and spent adequate time in God's Word, you will have a sound mind."[1]

We're back to the principles of chapter 4. God doesn't help

those who help themselves; he helps the helpless. "A bruised reed he will not break, and a smoldering wick he will not snuff out" (Is 42:3). Everything in our relationship with God must be grace first and grace-based. Everything in the church must be grace first and grace-based.

On the one hand, the church must never stop insisting that followers of Jesus become more and more like Jesus. The church must be relentless in its pursuit of holiness. That's the core of discipleship. But I'm just as passionate about the church being relentless in its pursuit of forgiveness and tireless in its acceptance of those who struggle to change.

I'm Not OK, You're Not OK

I've never been in a twelve-step program. We have a very successful one at our church, though. We call it New Wine, and we've helped dozens of other churches start similar programs. New Wine is church for the disenfranchised.

During any given week, we have four to five hundred people "in recovery," in support groups for special needs. We offer a catalog of unique opportunities for healing, from divorce recovery to anger management. Our church even hosts a support group for parents of murdered children. Based on the principles of the popular twelve-step programs, New Wine is an environment of unconditional love, acceptance, and forgiveness. And the people there have taught me a lot about myself and principles of Christian growth.

Have you ever heard someone in Alcoholics Anonymous

admit something like this: "I'm an alcoholic, but I haven't had a drink for six years, four months, and eight days." Does that trouble you? Do you believe that there are no alcoholics in the kingdom of God?

Then you may be part of the problem. You see, people in twelve-step programs are no different from anyone else, except perhaps they've had more serious personal difficulties. But that's the key. Speaking of the prostitute who bathed Jesus' feet with her tears and dried them with her hair, Jesus said, "I tell you, her many sins have been forgiven—for she loved much. But he who has been forgiven little loves little" (Lk 7:47).

People with serious problems have come to the end of themselves. Eugene Peterson captures this in his free translation of Romans 7:24: "I've tried everything and nothing helps. I'm at the end of my rope. Is there no one who can do anything for me?"

People with addictions have come face-to-face with their own absolute helplessness. They've discovered that the change that's always eluded them actually begins to occur when they acknowledge their vile dysfunction. So they keep confessing over and over that their weakness is real and persistent. That they are powerless to change themselves. That they need a "Higher Power." Isn't that the essential message of the Bible? Powerlessness: "All have sinned and fall short of the glory of God (Rom 3:23). Higher Power: "Believe on the Lord Jesus Christ and you will be saved" (Acts 16:31).

Letting Jesus Take Over

So the good news is that people really can change and do change! (Do you feel better now?) But the bitter irony is that profound change occurs *only* when God steps into our utterly debilitating weaknesses. I believe this is what Paul meant when he confessed, "Three times I pleaded with the Lord to take it away from me. But he said to me, 'My grace is sufficient for you, for my power is made perfect in weakness.' Therefore I will boast all the more gladly about my weaknesses, so that Christ's power may rest on me. That is why, for Christ's sake, I delight in weaknesses, in insults, in hardships, in persecutions, in difficulties. For when I am weak, then I am strong" (2 Cor 12:8-10).

Listen to the way Eugene Peterson renders this in *The Message:* "Three times I [begged God to remove it], and then he told me,

"'My grace is enough; it's all you need. My strength comes into its own in your weakness.'

"Once I heard that, I was glad to let it happen. I quit focusing on the handicap and began appreciating the gift. It was a case of Christ's strength moving in on my weakness. Now I take limitations in stride, and with good cheer, these limitations that cut me down to size—abuse, accidents, opposition, bad breaks. I just let Christ take over! And so the weaker I get, the stronger I become."

Emotional Disabilities

In the Scripture verse above, I'm drawn to Peterson's use of the term "handicap." It's still OK to use this word when you're talking about your bad golf game, but people who have physical limitations are not so likely to use it. I take that on the word of a dear friend, David, a paraplegic who has been educating me on these issues. He informed me that *handicap* has its roots in the "handy cap" that "crippled" people held out to collect change from passersby.

Disabled and *physically challenged* are much less demeaning terms. We are discovering that the physically challenged are people, too. Shamefully, I confess I was clueless about the issues of accessibility. I've even resented all the tax money it took to break up the corner curbs on sidewalks all around our city. *What for?* I'd ask myself silently. *I haven't seen any wheelchairs around here for years.* I used to feel this way, that is, until I started spending social time with David.

I've known people in wheelchairs. I've been kind to them. But all my personal friends were able-bodied. That's changing. I'm still way in the dark, but I've seen a burst of light.

I've experienced David's subculture firsthand. Watching his extraordinary effort—and waiting and waiting for him—to get in and out of his specially designed van. Pushing his wheelchair through a crowded basketball arena concourse. Standing in line for fast food. Getting in and out of restaurants. Sitting in the "accessible seating" deep in the end zone of an NFL game. Listening carefully to David's concerns when we designed our new worship center.

Barriers and unconscious prejudice are everywhere. And there's constant pain and distress: people who spend their lives in wheelchairs suffer in a myriad of ways unknown among physically healthy people. But times are changing. Slowly. And we've always known that men and women who are physically challenged can't just *will* themselves into health. We recognize that they have to learn how to accept their disability and make the best of life in spite of it.

We sort of understand. At least we try. At least we don't ask people in wheelchairs to play tackle football. But what about people with emotional problems? Are they "disabled"? Are they emotionally challenged? Or can they, should they, just shake themselves out of their anger or their gloom or their addiction?

They can do it if they try!

Or can they?

Loving the Emotionally Challenged

I have an idea for another book I hope to write sometime: *The D-Myth: Christians Are Never Supposed to Be Depressed or Discouraged, and If They Are, They Should Never Tell Anyone.*

I could speak with real insight on this subject. You see, I have a problem with depression as well as anger—no surprise, because the two emotions are often related. I have a family history of dark and brooding kinfolk. My dear uncle left full-time Christian ministry in his thirties because of chronic depression. He's been on permanent disability for more than thirty years.

Right this minute I'm not depressed. But depression can come on me as suddenly as a summer thunderstorm in Oklahoma. And I can't just shake it off. I can't just make it go away. Sometimes I feel as though I have no control over how I feel. I can't help myself.

Does my telling you these things alarm you? I confess, this kind of openness does pose certain risks. Every so often someone—usually someone new in our church—will quietly counsel me in the lobby after the service, "Pastor, I'm praying for you to be completely delivered from that spirit of depression." I just smile and tell them how grateful I am that they're concerned enough to pray for me personally.

But the reality is, I have prayed about it. Fasted for freedom from it. Received counsel and prayer for it. Read books about it. Preached about it. And now I'm writing about it because I know I am not alone in these struggles—these problems are pervasive in the church today (though they're seldom discussed).

"The prejudice against those with emotional problems," Dwight Carlson writes, "can be seen in churches across the nation on any Sunday morning. We pray publicly for the parishioner with cancer or a heart problem or pneumonia. But rarely will we pray publicly for Mary with severe depression, or Charles with incapacitating panic attacks, or the minister's son with schizophrenia. Our silence subtly conveys that these are not acceptable illnesses for Christians to have."[2]

No Excuses

My friend in the wheelchair, David, never complains. He's not bitter, or if he is, he's given me no clue. A graduate of the University of Arizona, he's a partner in a hugely successful microchip business here in Phoenix. Are you surprised? Did you picture him in some other way because earlier I told you he was in a wheelchair?

David is an extraordinary inspiration to me because he makes no excuses. David steadfastly refuses to let his disability get the best of him. Knowing that it's not just going to go away, he's done everything he can to live with it and live above it. And that's just how I feel about my emotional disabilities. I can't make them go away, but I'm not going to let them get the best of me either. How do I do that?

Self-Honesty Is the Best Policy

I like the language of twelve steppers: You can't make your problem go away, but you can manage it. You can keep it from getting the best of you, and you start by being brutally self-honest: "I have a problem with _____."

Does this sound like a "negative confession" to you? Surprise! This is biblical. Not only is it necessary for us to confess our sins to God, but "if we claim to be without sin, we deceive ourselves and the truth is not in us. If we confess ['continue to confess,' according to the original Greek] our sins, he is faithful and just and will forgive us our sins and purify us from all unrighteousness" (1 Jn 1:8-9).

The Healing Power of Confession

There are times when our healing awaits our willingness to confess our sins to trusted friends: "Confess your sins to each other and pray for each other so that you may be healed. The prayer of a righteous man is powerful and effective" (Jas 5:16).

Some of you will gnash your teeth at this one, but confession has always been an integral part of Catholic worship. It's one of the Catholic sacraments, right up there with baptism and Communion. In confession Catholics fully affirm the need to confess openly all our sins to another human being, who listens and reminds us of God's grace and forgiveness.

The Great Conflict

Is it any wonder we have so many unresolved issues among Bible-believing, born-again Christians? Our churches are not communities of open confession and healing grace. More often than not we have to hide from one another because we are so holiness-driven, so performance-oriented. But imagine the transformation that would be possible if the church became a place where I could meet Jesus "just as I am" *and* a place where people give me encouragement to grow and grace to fail.

I've found that my preaching is usually most effective when I let people see how Jesus heals and forgives my own areas of weakness. In order for me to point people to Jesus, like Paul I have to let them see Jesus bursting out of my weaknesses: "We have this treasure in jars of clay to show that this all-surpassing power is from God and not from us" (2 Cor 4:7).

Jesus is my Lord and Savior, but Paul is my hero. I want to be like Jesus, yet I feel more like Paul. He was, undoubtedly, what we call a Type A personality: high-energy, driven, impatient, opinionated, vocal. Sometimes combative. Yeah, I'm all those things. Paul was also frequently misunderstood. Me, too, although I can't say that I've provoked any municipal riots. Does getting loud at board meetings count?

So when Paul speaks, I listen. Jesus is my model of righteousness, and I follow him, but Paul is my model of how a man with explosive passions follows Jesus. "Follow my example," Paul wrote, "as I follow the example of Christ" (1 Cor 11:1).

Let's look, then, at what Paul says about his effort to become more like Christ in Romans 7. (Stay with me now. I've been making it easy for you, but you're going to have to think your way through the next couple of pages. You may have to break out your Bible and read Romans 7 a couple times.)

"I do not understand what I do," agonizes Paul. "For what I want to do I do not do, but what I hate I do. And if I do what I do not want to do, I agree that the law is good. As it is, it is no longer I myself who do it, but it is sin living in me. I know that nothing good lives in me, that is, in my sinful nature. For I have the desire to do what is good, but I cannot carry it out" (Rom 7:15-18).

This is the most difficult aspect of being a Christian. Now that you know what's right and wrong—and desire to serve God with all your heart—you discover that it just doesn't always work out that way. I call this the Great Conflict. It's a uniquely Christian predicament, because believers are painfully aware of the gaping gulf between who they are and what God says they should be.

Now this is not to say non-Christians have no conscience, but they certainly worry less about what God thinks about every little thing in life. Enviably, non-Christians seem to live in blissful ignorance of how far short of God's expectations they fall.

Most of them will tell you something like "I'm a pretty good person. Yeah, I have my faults, but I'm no worse a person than all those born-again Christians who claim to be so righteous." The Bible calls this a "seared conscience" (see 1 Tim 4:2). Now, not every unbeliever is a particularly "bad" person. They just don't lose any sleep over all their "little" sins.

We Christians are different. Like Paul, we desperately want to live for God but find that something inside keeps holding us back, and after a while, after years of trying to come out of that, we can feel a growing sense of condemnation: "So I find this law at work: When I want to do good, evil is right there with me. For in my inner being I delight in God's law; but I see another law at work in the members of my body, waging war against the law of my mind and making me a prisoner of the law of sin at work within my members. What a wretched man I am! Who will rescue me from this body of death?" (Rom 7:21-24).

Isn't that every person's desperate appeal? It's mine, and when I get to this in Romans 7, I'm saying to myself, *Yes! Yes! Paul is going to tell me! The explanation is about to unfold! The secret is about to be told! At last I'm going to break the bonds of earth and fly! Tell me, Paul, tell me!*

The answer is in verse 25: "Thanks be to God—through

Jesus Christ our Lord!" OK. So what else? Thanks be to God for *what*? Does Paul say Jesus is going to work a miracle and change me forever? What are you saying, Paul? Look at that verse again: "Thanks be to God—through Jesus Christ our Lord!" Is Paul really saying *anything* here?

Paul is giving thanks to God through Jesus, but he doesn't say specifically, "Thanks be to God because Jesus delivers me" or, "Thanks be to God, who delivers us through Jesus." That, in my opinion, would have been the perfect Christian conclusion to his argument. But Paul ends Romans 7 by boomeranging back to the problem and leaving us in the lurch: "So then, I myself in my mind am a slave to God's law, but in the sinful nature a slave to the law of sin."

The second half of the verse is like letting air out of a balloon. Read it again. Can you hear the sound effects? Inhale: "Thanks be to God—through Jesus Christ our Lord!" Exhale: "So then, I myself in my mind am a slave to God's law, but in the sinful nature a slave to the law of sin."

That's it?

That's just the way it is?

Is there no way out? No hope? The end of Romans 7 seems so vague, so unresolved, that Eugene Peterson's *The Message* puts words in Paul's mouth: "The answer, thank God, is that Jesus Christ can and does." But in fact, this is *not* what Paul said. It's what we *want* Paul to say, but he doesn't.

J.B. Phillips in *The New Testament in Modern English* does the same thing: "I thank God there is a way out through Jesus Christ our Lord." And I'm incredulous. J.B. Phillips ends Romans 7 right there. He leaves out the whole second half of the verse! How can he do that?

I'll tell you how. And why. Christians just can't bring themselves to accept the fact the war raging inside will not end in this life. That's why Paul says as a fact, "So then, I myself in my mind am a slave to God's law, but in the sinful nature a slave to the law of sin."

That's a reality, folks, that very few are willing to accept. Someone in a Christian twelve-step program might say it like this: "In my heart I'm a child of God, but in my sinful nature I always have been and always will be an alcoholic."

But is that all? Are we sentenced to live in the squalor of our sin forever? A thousand times no! Pay attention now: My hope is not that someday I won't have to worry about my anger, that someday, when I am spiritual enough, I will "arrive," and for the rest of this life I'll never have a major problem with anger or depression or whatever else anymore.

Instead, my hope is in Jesus, who continues to be my righteousness even when I'm unrighteous. In this life I'll always have a sense of falling short of what God expects of me, but the next sentence in Paul's discussion of the Great Conflict, like a cosmic cathedral bell, rings out a deafening declaration of assurance and hope: "Therefore, there is now no condemnation for those who are in Christ Jesus" (Rom 8:1).

Saved by Faith, Living by Faith

Let's put it all together: "What a wretched man I am! Who will rescue me from this body of death? Thanks be to God—

through Jesus Christ our Lord! So then, I myself in my mind am a slave to God's law, but in the sinful nature a slave to the law of sin. Therefore, there is now no condemnation for those who are in Christ Jesus" (Rom 7:24–8:1).

When is there no condemnation? Now! Right now, when you feel just like Paul, so wretchedly far from attaining the goal. But here is the irony of it all: When you give it up and tumble helplessly into the unconditional grace of God, just like all those twelve steppers, that's when you begin to change! That's when sin begins to lose its grip on your life.

This is what we Christians call living by faith. Yes, I'm *saved* by faith in the finished work of Christ. Most Christians have that one down pat. But I have to keep reminding myself that I'm *living* by faith in the finished work of Christ too. Paul, quoting the Old Testament prophet Haggai, announced, "The righteous will *live* by faith" (Gal 3:11).

"Abraham," Paul tells us in another extraordinary revelation of grace, "believed God, and it was credited to him as righteousness" (v. 6). Let me help you with that. Paul is saying, in effect, that when you place your trust in Christ, his perfect righteousness is given to you on credit, like a loan. When you buy a house, you use some rich guy's money. When he invests his money, it creates a pool of cash, which mortgage companies make available to people who have good credit. Simple enough.

When you become a Christian, when you're born again, all the righteousness of Christ is put into your account. You get Jesus on loan for the rest of your life. By faith, the righteousness of Jesus "on credit" keeps on making up for your daily righteousness deficit. Unlike the bank, though, Jesus gives us his good righteousness, even though we have terribly bad credit. And more, God's grace is so amazing that he doesn't ask for any payments. The righteousness of Christ is free—from start to finish.

That's why Paul could write in Romans 8: "Therefore, there is now no condemnation for those who are in Christ Jesus."

"So, what do you think? With God on our side like this, how can we lose? If God didn't hesitate to put everything on the line for us, embracing our condition and exposing himself to the worst by sending his own Son, is there anything else he wouldn't gladly and freely do for us? And who would dare tangle with God by messing with one of God's chosen? Who would dare to even point a finger? The One who died for us!—who was raised to life for us!—is in the presence of God at this very moment sticking up for us.

"Do you think anyone is going to be able to drive a wedge between us and Christ's love for us? There is no way! Not trouble, nor hard times, not hatred, not hunger, not homelessness, not bullying threats, not backstabbing, not even the worst sins listed in Scripture.... None of this fazes us because Jesus loves us. I'm absolutely convinced that nothing—living or dead, angelic or demonic, today or tomorrow, high or low, thinkable or unthinkable—absolutely *nothing* can get between us and God's love because of the fact that Jesus our Master has embraced us" (Rom 8:31-39, *The Message*).

I'm determined to live by faith in God's relentless, measureless, incomprehensible, unconditional love for me, and I'm not going to hang my life on the hope that someday I'll never have any more problems. That day is called heaven, and until I get to heaven, I'm not going to trust in my wobbly, wavering goodness. "I no longer live, but Christ lives in me. The life I live in the body, I live by faith in the Son of God, who loved me and gave himself for me" (Gal 2:20).

This fills me with such hope that my depression is, well, gone. I don't feel even slightly angry. And I didn't need a lobotomy either.

....

Holy and Merciful God: You know me, inside and out. You know what I'm struggling with inside, and you accept me fully, knowing that I will never be perfect in this lifetime. There is now no condemnation in your heart for me. You accept me, so I will accept myself. Amen.

....

....

EIGHT

Misbelief 8:

If Something Bad Happens, It Must Mean There's Something Bad in Me

Your Father in heaven ... causes his sun to rise on the evil and the good, and sends rain on the righteous and the unrighteous.

MATTHEW 5:45

*O*verheard in a church prayer group far, far away....

"Are there any other prayer requests?"

A hesitant voice pipes up, "How about Rosemary?"

"We've been praying for Rosemary's cancer for six months now. It's so frustrating. Why isn't she being healed?"

"I don't understand it either. We prayed that God would provide for our new furnace, and he came through. We asked him for good weather for our father-son barbecue, and there wasn't a cloud in the sky. God has always answered our prayers before."

"It hurts to see her like this.... We've been praying so hard! And now the doctors have told her there is nothing they can do. I haven't been to visit her in weeks. I just don't know what to say!"

"Maybe ... well, I hate to say it, but maybe some sort of sin in her life is holding back God's healing hand."

"Rosemary? She's a wonderful wife and mother!"

"Who knows? Something is preventing the healing, and we know it's not us!"

Kathy, the young wife of one of our pastors, died suddenly of an E. coli infection three weeks after giving birth to her third child. Some people in our congregation hinted that our church wasn't "spiritual" enough. Maybe she died because God was judging our church for something.

They actually thought God would take the life of a young mother to get our attention? That's right. Some "spiritually minded" Christian actually said that! The title of this book is *Dumb Things Smart Christians Believe.* "Dumb" is too nice a word to use to describe that kind of "spirituality."

And yet it's rampant. People think like that all the time. Job's friends were no exception, and the disciples once asked Jesus about a blind man, "Rabbi, who sinned, this man or his parents, that he was born blind?" (Jn 9:2).

"Neither," Jesus said.

Searching in Vain for Answers

Kathy came to our church as a single mom. She had her first child out of wedlock, and the first Sunday she attended Word of Grace was Mother's Day. That weekend I went out on a limb (who, me?) and preached specifically about the challenges of single parenting in order to affirm those who were raising their children alone. Kathy said to herself, *This church is for me.*

Within a year she applied for a position on our church staff and met Jeff, one of our pastors and a single dad with the custody of two kids. They fell in love, and I did their wedding. A few years later they had Adam, their first child together, and then just two years ago this fall, Kathy gave birth to their second child, little Ben.

It was a Thursday, just two weeks after Ben was born, when Kathy was stricken with excruciating back pain. Jeff raced her to the hospital, but the staff in the emergency room, thinking it was a kidney stone or something else not so serious, sent her home.

Friday she was worse, and Jeff took her back to the hospital. It was too late. Wednesday morning Kathy died of E. coli poisoning.

It makes me cry again just to tell the story.

One week later we had a service, the largest attendance ever for any funeral I'd done. What did I say to them? What would you have said?

Why would something like this happen to one of the most likable—and godly—couples in our congregation? Why was Kathy taken from Jeff, now the single father of *five* children, the youngest an infant who would never know his mother?

This was not the first time Jeff had grappled with such devastating loss either. As a teenager, Jeff had watched his father die in his arms; one of his brothers was murdered; another committed suicide; and he lost his first wife under extraordinarily difficult circumstances. And yet if you met Jeff today, he wouldn't give you a clue that his life has been so filled with tragedy. He's kept the faith.

So, what would you say at Kathy's funeral service? To Jeff? To Kathy's parents? To her sister? To all the people in our church who were soul-searching, looking for answers, waiting for wisdom? As a pastor, I face these tough questions time after time, but it never gets easier. Often it just breaks my heart a little more.

It was Thanksgiving Day 1998. Walt and Lori were celebrating the holiday at their mountain cabin. Scott and Marlene, who had just lost a child to leukemia, were spending the weekend with them.

"Turkey's ready!" Lori informed the gang outside.

Although he knew it was about time to eat, Scott may not have heard her. He was giving little Ashli, Walt and Lori's adorable two-year-old, one last ride on his go-cart. Inside the cabin Lori and Marlene heard a horrific crash. Somehow Scott had lost control and crashed into his pickup parked along the graveled forest lane.

In a panic Walt ran out to the front of the cabin. There was Scott, sitting on the road in shock, in pain. Ashli was lying on the go-cart, unconscious from a severe head injury. She died a few hours later.

I did that funeral too. What would you have said to Walt and Lori? To Scott, who had just lost a child, and now *this!* Is there a God? Why do such bad things happen to such good people?

This is, almost word for word, what I said:

This is as bad as it gets. We are not here today to pretend it's any other way. This is absolutely every parent's worst nightmare, and you, Walt and Lori, are living that nightmare.

Lori, when you walked through this same terrible misfortune with Scott and his wife, as they lost their child, you were wondering, thinking, "How can they cope with this?" Now we're wondering that about you and Walt: "How are they going to survive this?"

No matter how much we try to feel what you are feeling, there is no way anyone standing on the outside can even begin to understand what you two are going through on the inside— not grandparents, not brothers or sisters. No one. Right now you are experiencing the kind of loss and grief that experts talk about as something utterly unique, and no one can know what it's like unless they experience it for themselves. And none of us wants to. Secretly, we're all grateful that it was not one of our children.

This is as bad as it gets.

My own daughter just turned twenty-one, and she's finishing college in three weeks. I bought her a car on Friday, her first car. Yesterday, she purchased her own auto insurance policy. You know, Walt and Lori, I had this terrible sinking feeling inside. She's going to be living in California. Today she's interviewing for a job, and she'll be commuting forty-five minutes every day on the freeways in L.A. What do you think went through my mind?

And every family here, you're thinking about your children, your grandchildren, aren't you? Yes, this is as bad as it gets. There is nothing worse than losing a child. Walt and Lori, I just can't imagine what you are feeling right now. What you are going to feel for the next year, even years from now.

I need to tell you something, to help you face the reality of all this. What you are feeling now is not going to go away. You will try to make it go away, try to forget, but you won't.

All the sincere, well-meaning people in your life will try to make it go away for you, but no one will be able to say just the right thing that will change how you feel. No one among the hundreds of people in this room will come up with just the right clever, insightful thing to say so that you'll respond, "Thank you! That's just what I was waiting to hear. I'm OK now."

Only God can help you through this, and I am certain he will.

Are the rest of you listening to me? You can't fix this problem. You can't fix Walt and Lori. You can be instruments of God's love. You can pray for them. But you can't make their pain and sadness disappear.

Four Important Facts About Grief

How can it be that all things work together for good for those who love God? When something really bad like this happens, does it mean there's something really bad in me?

If you are asking yourself these questions, I have four thoughts for you to consider.

1. Jesus Doesn't Answer All Our Questions
In the Gospel of Luke we read of a curious incident in the life of Jesus.

"Now there were some present at that time who told Jesus about the Galileans whose blood Pilate had mixed with their sacrifices. Jesus answered, 'Do you think that these Galileans were worse sinners than all the other Galileans because they suffered this way? I tell you, no! But unless you repent, you too will all perish. Or those eighteen who died when the tower in Siloam fell on them—do you think they were more guilty than all the others living in Jerusalem? I tell you, no! But unless you repent, you too will all perish'" (Lk 13:1-5).

Times were terrible. Palestine was under the iron fist of the Roman Empire, and there were many Jewish people who expected the Messiah to come at any moment and overthrow the brutal Roman occupational government. A few Jews even participated in covert revolutionary activities, and according to this passage, some apparently were captured and executed.

A heartless man, Pontius Pilate, the Roman governor who would one day order Jesus to be crucified, mixed the blood of those martyrs with the blood of the Jewish animal sacrifices. To the Hebrew people, this was an outrage, an abomination.

So, Jesus, what do *you* think about all this? Why did this happen to these people? Were they bad people?

Jesus answered them and us, "Do you think that these people were worse sinners than other people because they suffered this way?" And then, to refute this idea, Jesus came back at them with his own example of random suffering and meaningless death, the eighteen who died at the tower of Siloam.

Still, we continue to ask, why? Why *these* people, and why *this* way? Why do such bad things happen to such good people and innocent children? Why Ashli?

Here are the standard answers, often offered by those who mean well and don't know what else to say.

This was an act of God! That's what the insurance companies call it. But privately we wonder how God could be responsible for such terrible things.

The devil did this! You know, sometimes he just snakes his way outside the sovereignty of God.

This was caused by something we did. God is punishing us. The only reasonable explanation is that bad things happen when people are bad. Or maybe you just didn't pray long enough during your family devotions that day. Did you pray at all?

To me, this bizarre, relatively unknown passage in Luke 13 is one of the most important in all the Bible because it records Jesus' answer to the universal question: "Why did this happen?"

Are you sitting on the edge of your seat? Here's his answer: "Or those eighteen who died when the tower in Siloam fell on them—do you think they were more guilty than all the others living in Jerusalem? I tell you, no! But unless you repent, you too will all perish."

Jesus doesn't answer the question! Well, at least he doesn't answer it the way any of us would. He doesn't write it off as an act of God. He doesn't blame the devil. In fact, he doesn't even mention the devil. And he clearly rules out the possibility that these were bad people. Were they? Jesus is emphatic: "I tell you, no!"

So, where does that leave us? Well, if Jesus Christ, the Son of God, doesn't propose a philosophical or theological commentary on tragic loss of life, I'm not going to either. Jesus offers no explanation, but he does give a response that highlights the meaning for the people still alive who are asking the question (not the meaning of why this happened to the people who died): "But unless you repent, you too will all perish."

What I believe Jesus is telling us here is that tragedies in life get our attention. Because some circumstances in life are profoundly troubling, they cause us to ask all the most important questions about the meaning of life and death and relationship with God, and they remind us, sometimes savagely, how human life is a precious gift and altogether fragile. How the only thing that matters in the end is whether or not we have a relationship with God. Jesus doesn't answer all our questions, but he offers himself. Can you believe?

2. The World Is a Mess

This blue planet of ours is wondrous. Spectacular beauty. Life-forms of inexplicable intricacy and complexity.

And hellish suffering.

It's a breathtaking world of pain and death.

Human beings contribute to our planet's wonder. Created in the image of God, we are its highest life-form. We are also capable of unspeakable horror. Human beings make mistakes and do stupid things, everything from dialing wrong phone numbers to running red lights. Some of the dumb things we do are inconsequential. Other times we make mistakes that haunt us for a lifetime. A small error in judgment on the part of one man killed a little girl.

And then there's all the other stuff that happens, things for which human beings are not responsible and over which we have no control, like floods and earthquakes and collapsing buildings. There's a Bible verse for this: "We know that the whole creation has been groaning as in the pains of childbirth right up to the present time. Not only so, but we ourselves, who have the firstfruits of the Spirit, groan inwardly as we wait eagerly for our adoption as sons, the redemption of our bodies" (Rom 8:22-23).

This world is not our home. My father died of mylodysplasia, a blood disease, one month before Dad and Mom's fiftieth wedding anniversary. My whole family suffered through the trauma of his disease. Everything inside of us groaned. At that time the world was not orderly or predictable; it was full of frustration and pain. Here's why: "For the creation was subjected to frustration, not by its own choice, but by the will of the one who subjected it, in hope that the creation itself will be liberated from its bondage to decay and brought into the glorious freedom of the children of God" (Rom 8:20-21).

This world is not heaven. This world is cursed, but we live like it isn't. We have unrealistic expectations, even illusions, about what life in this world should give us, so when something terrible like this happens, when the little Ashlis around us are ripped away, we're in shock. Not that Ashli's kind of death should be common, but we forget that the Bible keeps reminding us about the frailty of human life and that we are living, right now, in a world that's under the curse of sin and death.

3. All Things Work Together for Good

"We know that in all things God works for the good of those who love him, who have been called according to his purpose"

(Rom 8:28). In *all* things? In Ashli's life and death, too?

Yes, in all things. That's Paul's whole point. According to Romans 8, all things work together for good right here on planet earth, where the whole creation is groaning under the curse of sin. "All things work together for good" is often a flippant remark you hear from Christians who don't know what else to say to someone who's going through hell. But for Paul, here in Romans 8, it's our grand hope in a cursed, hopeless world.

In her incredible little book, *A Window to Heaven: When Children See Life in Death*, Diane Komp, professor of pediatrics at Yale University, describes her experiences as a pediatric oncologist living with dying children. By her own admission in an interview for *Life* magazine, earlier in her life she was an atheist at worst and an agnostic at best. But after living with and studying these children, she became a Christian believer. Why? Because she saw incontestable evidence of God in miracles of living and dying among her patients.

Life out of death. Light in the darkness. All things work for good, even when there's evil.

A few hours before Kathy died of the E. coli infection, her family brought each of her five children into her hospital room to say good-bye. Kathy was unconscious, but the children had a chance to share a final moment with their mommy.

What happened next was, perhaps, the most extraordinary spiritual phenomenon I've encountered in twenty-five years of Christian ministry. I wasn't present, but Kathy's brother-in-law, a cautious physician, witnessed the event and tearfully shared it with me.

"From where we were standing together, waiting for the elevator, you could look back through a large window and see the outside of the window to Kathy's room.

"Well, we had just been in to see Kathy for the last time, and were all standing there in the hall waiting for the elevator. I was carrying Adam (just two-and-a-half years old), who suddenly pointed directly out the window to his mother's room and shrieked, 'There's Jesus!'"

4. There Is No Obstacle to God's Love

The love of God does not keep us away from suffering, but our suffering—no matter what we suffer or how we suffer—can never keep us away from the love of God. Look once more at Romans 8:

"Who shall separate us from the love of Christ? Shall trouble or hardship or persecution or famine or nakedness or danger or sword? ... No, in all these things we are more than conquerors through him who loved us. For I am convinced that neither death nor life, neither angels nor demons, neither the present nor the future, nor any powers, neither height nor depth, nor anything else in all creation, will be able to separate us from the love of God that is in Christ Jesus our Lord" (Rom 8:35-39).

Nothing will separate us.... When you're angry with God, when you don't feel like praying, when you don't feel like being spiritual, God is going to keep loving you.

"For your sake," Paul writes, "we are considered as sheep to be slaughtered" (v. 36). Paul isn't just talking theory here. Having come very close to death several times himself, he knew how dangerous it could be to follow Jesus. Before meeting Christ himself, he had participated in the killing of other Christians.

So when Paul declares that "all things work for good," he's not just saying, "Oh, you can learn some good lessons about life when you're going through tough times, like when you have a flat tire or you miss an important appointment." No, Paul is teaching us that good can come out of the worst imaginable things in the worst imaginable world.

Look again at the key verses of Romans 8: "For the creation was subjected to frustration.... And we know that in all things God works for the good of those who love him.... [Nothing] in all creation, will be able to separate us from the love of God that is in Christ Jesus our Lord."

The Problem With People on Planet Earth

Peter and the early Christians had a very different perspective than our comfortable lifestyle gives us: "Dear friends, do not be surprised at the painful trial you are suffering, as though something strange were happening to you. But rejoice that you participate in the sufferings of Christ, so that you may be overjoyed when his glory is revealed" (1 Pt 4:12-13).

Paul confirms this. "What I mean, brothers, is that the time is short. From now on those who have wives should live as if they had none; those who mourn, as if they did not; those who are happy, as if they were not; those who buy something, as if it were not theirs to keep; those who use the things of the world, as if not engrossed in them. For this world in its present form is passing away" (1 Cor 7:29-31).

We Christians today have an obsession with our own happiness. We've grown to believe that God is on our side, that he will do everything he can to bless us and to protect us from pain and suffering.

That kind of God can't be found in the writings of the early church. God wasn't there to keep them out of suffering or to take their suffering away. God was there to sustain them through their suffering. The early Christians were much less likely than us to wonder why bad things happen to good people. They believed bad things happened to them *because* they were good!

So Peter wrote, "It is commendable if a man bears up under the pain of unjust suffering because he is conscious of God. But how is it to your credit if you receive a beating for doing wrong and endure it? But if you suffer for doing good and you endure it, this is commendable before God. To this you were called, because Christ suffered for you, leaving you an example, that you should follow in his steps" (1 Pt 2:19-21).

Comfort and the Cross

If Jesus appeared to you right now, if he stood right there in front of you, placed his strong and gentle hand on your shoulder, and whispered softly, "Everything is going to be all right," would you believe him? Would you feel comfort and peace? Would you, for a moment, forget everything else?

Well, he did. In the Bible. Can you hear his voice? "I know you can't see it now, but all of this is going to work together for good."

Hold your Bible in your hands.

Jesus said it, right here in that big, floppy book.

"Everything is going to be OK."

Loving Father: Today I have a hard time feeling anything, least of all your love. It is hard to be conscious of anything but the unbelievable pain and gut-wrenching loss at times like this. But I believe you are there—not to spare me from going through it but to guide me to the other side. Help me to keep my eyes on you and not look to others for the answers. Amen.

....

NINE

Misbelief 9:

Being Spiritual Is All That Matters, Because It's All That Matters to God

"...which we have heard, which we have seen with our eyes, which we have looked at and our hands have touched..."

1 JOHN 1:1

Conversation between a missionary on furlough and an elder of a supporting church....

"So, Jim, what is it that you're doing out there in ... where is it, Africa?"

"Senegal, West Africa. My primary responsibility is to run an English-speaking school..."

"What do you teach? Bible classes?"

"No, math and science mostly. It's what I'm good at."

"Oh. What about after class? Do you go into the villages and evangelize the natives?"

"Well, Dakar is a pretty modern city. Sometimes I go and play basketball in the courtyard with a few young men who live nearby."

"As a way to reach them for the Lord, no doubt."

"Mainly just to get exercise after sitting at a desk all day!

Most of the young men already belong to the church we attend."

"'Attend'? You're not the pastor?"

"No, a local pastor is now in charge."

"Imagine that! Well, what about your wife?"

"She runs things at home. It's a full-time job, even with help. Just going to the market is an all-day excursion. Plus she's learning the language and running her ladies' crafts class."

"She has a maid? And she teaches crafts? My, that doesn't sound too fruitful for the kingdom! Missionaries are supposed to concentrate on winning souls!"

What would you have said if you had been that missionary?

The "Sacred" and the "Secular"

Is it true that "spiritual" things are better, more important than "natural" things?

Is praying or reading the Bible always more important than, say, eating? Or mowing the grass? Or cleaning the house?

Is going to church a "higher," more excellent activity than working or going to a ball game?

Many Christians would answer yes to each question. Their exaggerated opinion of "spiritual" things is a misbelief they hold dear. And it's one that comes into play in many ways as they seek to balance "things seen" and "things unseen" in their lives. Here are a few ways it trips up a lot of people.

"'Spiritually minded' people have an edge over those who just use their 'natural minds.'"

I run into this one all the time. Every church seems to have its core of "ultra-spiritual" people, whom I affectionately refer to as "The Deeper Life Club." These well-meaning folks are usually very dedicated to Jesus and pray earnestly for the church. On the other hand, their comments often leave me feeling as though I am not spiritual enough to be their pastor. They leave others feeling spiritually inadequate, too, and they tend to spiritualize just about everything. Every decision we make at the church needs to be bathed in prayer, I'm told. Yes, every one of several hundred daily decisions.

These people are really troubled when I tell them that, most of the time, we just fly (sometimes stumble) from one demand to the next, based on what seems right at the time. In a large church (and in small ones too!), there aren't enough hours in the day to pray a specific prayer over every little thing, like whether or not it's time to get new curtains for the nursery.

A few years ago, when we decided to build our new two thousand-seat worship center, several people raised the question, "Is this *really* what God wants us to do?" When that came up in a meeting, one very pragmatic board member replied, "Right now we have to do six worship services every weekend. I think that's a sign from God that we should consider building." In other words, sometimes the will of God is pretty clear without a lot of spiritualizing.

Oh, we pray at our church! We prayed a lot about our new worship center, too! I have my own P.I.T. Crew (Personal

Intercessory Team), who are praying for me right now as I'm writing this book. And yet, right now I'm not praying over every page. I'm just letting it flow out of the gift God has given me to write.

Let's take a look at a few more common misconceptions many Christians have about "spiritual" and "natural."

"Pastors and elders should do spiritual ministry; deacons should handle everyday things."

Certainly the Bible urges Christian leaders to delegate particular tasks to qualified people in the church, so that pastors and prophets can give their "attention to prayer and the ministry of the word" (Acts 6:4). But watch out! If you're not careful, a wrong application of this is the stuff of religious hierarchy and elitism.

Nowhere in Acts 6, where we read how the early leaders of the church selected administrative assistants for the first time, is there any suggestion that the appointees were lesser men. We need to esteem people in "the ministry" for their hard work, but that doesn't mean they're better or more spiritual.

I am by profession a clergyman, which means that God has given me the ability to dig meaningful insights out of the Bible and to communicate those principles to large numbers of people. However, this fact doesn't elevate me to a special class in the caste system of the kingdom. I expect respect; I hate to be idolized. Too much honor and pastors become untouchable.

All of us in the church are partners in kingdom business

together: "From [Christ] the whole body, joined and held together by every supporting ligament grows and builds itself up in love, as each part does its work" (Eph 4:16). As I read it, that's everybody.

"We shouldn't be running this church like a business."

Is running a church like a business *unspiritual?* Is business *unspiritual?* If we don't run the church "like a business," using sound business practices, how should we run it?

The business office at my church counts and accounts for the money given and spent in the church, and we have it audited annually. We have an employee manual that's consistent with labor laws. We have salary ranges and salary reviews, and we issue over two hundred W-2s every year. We also have formal retirement plans for our employees. We own property: land and buildings, computers, desks, and office supplies. (Smaller churches have all the same stuff, just less of it.)

In short, we're a business. There's nothing "unspiritual" about that. If there were, why would Paul have sandwiched administration[1] right there between healing and speaking in tongues in the parade of *spiritual* gifts (see 1 Cor 12:28)? In this same chapter Paul unfolds his landmark teaching on the body of Christ, how every member is important and necessary regardless of function. Every member has a "spiritual" function.

I can't recall hearing of a single instance where a church failed because of good business practices. On the other hand,

I've seen a fair share of churches get into financial trouble because they *didn't* run their ministry like a business. Of course, a church that merely practices sound business principles may not be as effective in evangelism or outreach. On the other hand, when a local church does not conduct itself according to sound business principles, the ministry is bound to suffer in other areas as well.

To illustrate, recently we brought a new associate pastor on to our church staff. He was unemployed when we interviewed him, because he had chosen to resign, along with the rest of the church ministry staff at his former church. The senior pastor there had a serious moral failure, and against the counsel of the elders and other local pastors, refused to step down.

Shortly after accepting the new position at our church, our business administrator handed our new associate a copy of our comprehensive employee manual. At first read, he was troubled by our strict policies, but later, he told me, he called some of his friends from his former church to tell them, "If we had had an employee manual like Word of Grace, we would have spared our church much of the crisis that eventually destroyed it."

Churches are often very casual about the way they do business, so when a serious problem arises, they have no system to guide them through the crisis to resolution and healing. As we allow the "business" side of church to support the "spiritual" side, the entity as a whole is strengthened.

"People in the ministry don't live like other people."

A member of our church recently bumped into me at a baseball card shop. His greeting to me was "So *this* is what happens to our tithe money."

Truly!

It wasn't the first time something like that has happened to me. One time a woman in our church was surprised to see me in the garden shop at K-Mart. I was "Saturday dirty," but that's not what she noticed first. "Pastor Kinnaman," she blurted out in surprise as she stepped back away from my holy space, "I've never seen your legs before!" (I think she meant, "This is the first time I've seen you in shorts.")

And then there was the time a friend of ours came to see our new home. When she stepped into the master bath, she yelled back at me, "So this is where the man of God goes to the bathroom!" She was just being funny, but the thought did cross her mind. Would you think about that? I mean, when you're at a friend's home and ask to use their bathroom, do you think about *them* using it?

Probably not. Nor would you think twice if you saw a friend at the baseball store or in shorts at K-Mart. Everyone knows that men of God don't use the bathroom, buy deodorant, or wear shorts in public, right?

Here's another one: People in the ministry don't have sex. The highly regarded *Leadership Journal* asked pastors to submit stories of ridiculous things that had happened to them in the ministry. One clergyman and his wife had several adopted children. When this fact came to the attention of one dear older woman, she whispered softly to her pastor one day, "It's really better when ministers have children *that* way."

The idea that pastors and others in ministry are somehow different in how they live their daily lives is one of those "spiritual misbeliefs" that drive me nuts: if God is a spiritual being who relates to us on a spiritual level, then those of us who represent him should relate to people primarily on a spiritual level.

"Oh, Pastor Gary, you are so human!" I've heard it dozens of times. Why would people say that? Is it unusual for a pastor to be human? Or are they implying that "spiritual" and "human" are essentially incompatible? In other words, the more spiritual I am, the less human I'll be, and the more human I am, the less spiritual I'll be?

When people tell me that I'm so human, I tell them I have no idea what else to be. And I tell them about Jesus, who was fully human.

God took human flesh into his own nature. And in doing so, in the Person of Jesus, God became human. This is what we refer to as the doctrine of the Incarnation, a theological term derived from the Latin for "in flesh." The Incarnation was the "enfleshment" of God.

Furthermore, when the Father raised Jesus from the dead, it wasn't just a spiritual resurrection. His physical body came out of the grave and later ascended into heaven. Right now Jesus is seated at the right hand of the Father. God, then, not only became flesh for the thirty-three years of Jesus' human life, but he took that human flesh back into himself forever.

It's Good to Be Human!

Humanity is good. Long before Adam sinned, he was fully human, and though Adam certainly had a spiritual focus, he was not a spirit being. He was a *human* being. Jesus did not come to deliver us from our humanity but to deliver our humanity from the curse and power of sin, from the abuse of our humanity.

Jesus came to make our humanity holy. *Holy* means, simply, "set apart for God," not "less human." When I became a Christian, I didn't become less human; my humanity became more godly.

Holy doesn't mean better; it just means set apart. When I bless our family dinner, my prayer doesn't improve on my wife's great home cooking. It just means that we are recognizing that our food comes from God, and we are acknowledging that our time together as a family is special.

Every word we speak, not just Christian thoughts or Bible words spoken with a religious tone—everything we say belongs to God. Which also means that we probably won't say the things we would say if we didn't belong to God. Whatever we do, even if it's as common a thing as eating and drinking, we're to do for the glory of God.

Because There Is a God, Everything Matters

When my future son-in-law, Jeff, and my daughter, Shari, were home from California for a weekend to begin preparing for their wedding, we had a chat about this. A second-year seminary student, Jeff is a very bright guy. He acknowledged that, for the last couple of years, he's been struggling to find some middle ground in his life.

"I used to think," he told me over tacos (my daughter and my wife were doing wedding stuff), "that the best way to spend the day was to pray as long as I could and read the Bible as much as I could, to devote myself fully to 'the things of God.' But some of my reading lately has changed the way I think."

"Really?"

He nodded. "Are you familiar with the views of Madeleine L'Engle?" he asked.

"No," I admitted unwillingly. (I hate it when my kids know stuff I should know!)

"She says," Jeff informed me, "that there are, essentially, two ways to look at life. One: there is a God; therefore, nothing else matters. Two: there is a God; therefore, everything matters. I've been moving more toward the second view," Jeff added.

So, is God as interested in my baseball card collection as he is in my writing this book? He is!

The perfect father is interested in every little thing going on in his kids' lives. I have three children. I pray for them to walk with God, for Jesus to be Lord of their lives, for them to honor and obey God's Word. But my wife, Marilyn, and I are also compulsively interested in everything else about them—so much so that sometimes we drive them crazy!

Nothing About You Is Trivial to God

Here's a trivia question: What's the very first question, according to the Gospel of John, that the disciples asked Jesus when they all first met? We could imagine a few. "What's heaven like?" "What's the secret to your miracle-working power?" "How many angels can stand on the head of a pin?" But no, none of that.

What they asked Jesus seems trivial to us now: "Rabbi, where are you staying?" (Jn 1:38). Some translations have it, "Where do you live?" (Everybody wants to know where the pastor lives, now, don't they?) "Where do you live?" What kind of simpleton would ask the Son of God a superficial question like that?

Do you know how Jesus responded? It's in the next verse: "Come and see." In other words, Jesus was saying, "I'm for real. What you see is what you get." The religious community would stumble over his humanity. Because they couldn't perceive his full deity in his full humanity, they crucified him for blasphemy.

Platonic Christians

So, if Jesus was fully human, and if God loves our body as much as our soul, where did this spiritual-versus-natural stuff come from?

You can trace it back to Plato and the Greek worldview he represented. The idea of an incarnation—God taking on human flesh—was repugnant to the Greeks because they believed that the reality of the material world was secondary to that of the spiritual, or what the ancient Greeks called the world of ideals. The ideals (the spiritual side of life) was everything, and matter just didn't matter much.

Paul ran into this when he preached on Mars Hill in Athens, an event recorded in Acts 17. His listeners were seriously interested in his novel views until Paul said the inconceivable: "God has given proof of what I'm preaching to all men by raising Jesus from the dead" (see v. 31).

"When they heard about the resurrection of the dead," Luke reports, "some of them sneered" (v. 32). Why? Such a thing was unthinkable for them. In the Greek worldview, death was the long-anticipated release of a person's spirit from the prison of the body.

This Greek idea (matter is evil; spirit is good) started dribbling into Christian teaching before the end of the first century, when the apostles John and Paul were still writing portions of the New Testament. This early heresy was called Gnosticism, taken from the Greek word for knowledge and knowing, because the Gnostics prided themselves in their spiritual revelation and knowledge.

In Gnosticism ("knowingism") the only way you could know God was by pressing into a higher knowledge and a deeper spiritual revelation. The material world was meaningless, so it didn't really matter if you honored your relationships, worked your job responsibly, or helped your neighbor. Being spiritual was all that mattered.

So John counters, "We know that we have come to know him if we obey his commands. The man who says, 'I know him' [the Gnostic, of course], but does not do what he commands is a liar" (1 Jn 2:3-4). John is telling us that, if you say you're a Christian, you need to act like one. Sometimes that means getting down and dirty.

To use a worn cliché, Gnostics were too heavenly minded to be any earthly good, unlike Jesus, who was down to earth, flesh and blood. That's why John opened his first letter with a forceful appeal to the humanity of Christ: "That which was from the beginning [that is, Jesus Christ], which we have seen with our eyes, which we have looked at and our hands have touched—this we proclaim concerning the Word of life" (1 Jn 1:1).

Many world religions, in one way or another, teach that the spiritual, immaterial world is good and the material world is evil. Generally, religion is a universal quest, the sharp focus of human effort, to lift oneself higher, to penetrate the divine, to escape the clutches of time and space and fly to worlds unknown, even to be reincarnated into a higher caste. There is a God, so a lot of people believe that nothing else matters.

Except the God of the Bible created matter and life. And said it was good. And then he created human life and purposely placed us here to work and to enjoy his creation. God's goal is not to get us out of here but to get himself back in. Not to destroy creation but to restore it. Not to release me from the limitation of my humanity but to release my humanity from the deadly limitations and consequences of sin.

God is good. After he made everything, God said, "That's good too." I agree with my daughter's husband, Jeff: there is a God; therefore, everything matters. Being spiritual has nothing to do with acting spiritual. True spirituality is bringing Jesus into every activity, from going to church to family vacations—and asking him to bless it by joining you.

True spirituality is being full of heaven and down to earth.

True spirituality is being just like Jesus.

"There are sacred jobs and secular jobs."

You may have heard of the best-selling book *Experiencing God* by Henry Blackaby and Claude King. These two men just released another book, *The Power of the Call*, which I purchased and tucked into my travel bag to read on a personal retreat. The book is loaded with instructive and encouraging material for people like myself in "full-time ministry."

And yet I was disappointed with one of the key themes in the book: the idea that "the ministry" is greater than any other vocation. The authors write, "No one else in society has a greater or higher calling," and this "is an incredible call, unequaled by any other vocation."[2]

There was a time when I would have responded with a loud "Amen," because this view is very commonly held among both those who are in "the ministry" and those who are not. Unfortunately, this idea makes an idol of "the ministry" and takes the edge off the blessing of God on "secular work." It's also not exactly biblical.

"The ministry" is a special vocation, no doubt. I'm in the ministry. But I must argue that it's not the "highest calling," that it's not somehow better than any other "job." The popular notion that "the ministry" is in a job classification all its own is based on the commonly held distinction between the secular and the sacred, which we are hard-pressed to find in the Bible. The idea, though, goes all the way back to the very earliest years of Christian history.

The first church historian, Eusebius, argued that Christ gave "two ways" to his church. One is the "perfect life" (the ministry); the other is "permitted" (or "secular" jobs). In the next few centuries both Augustine and Thomas Aquinas picked up on this theme by elevating the "contemplative life"—a matter of freedom—over the "active life"—a matter of necessity.[3]

What most people don't know is that this distinction between holy and unholy was one of the key issues of the Protestant Reformation. It is commonly known that Martin Luther reshaped Christian thinking with two ideas: (1) salvation is by grace alone (Jesus plus nothing); and (2) the Bible alone is the source of Christian doctrine and our authority for life. Less known, and what may be Luther's greatest contribution to social history, was his idea of labor.

Before Luther, work was generally viewed as a necessary evil, and people pretty much worked to survive. Like a pride of lions on the hunt, people lived, literally, hand to mouth. Families grew only enough grain and raised only enough livestock to provide for their own personal needs.

Luther changed all that by introducing what we now call "the Protestant work ethic." All work is sacred, Luther taught, and "the ministry" is no more sacred than any other vocation. When you work in your field or in a workshop, look around you, Luther told the people in his church. Your work and the tools of your trade—your hammer, your plow, your pots and pans (nowadays your computer keyboard!)—are gifts from God for you to serve others, not just to provide for yourself.

"The works of priests and pastors," Luther wrote, "however holy and arduous they be, do not differ one whit in the sight of God from the works of the laborer in the field or the woman going about her household tasks."[4]

A Bible illustration of this is the story of Moses tending sheep in the wilderness of Sinai. It was there that the Lord appeared to him in the burning bush.

"What's that in your hand?" God asked.

"A shepherd's staff," Moses replied.

"Throw it on the ground," God commanded him.

Immediately it became a serpent. The common tool of Moses' trade was the most spiritual object of the moment, but Moses didn't have a clue (see Ex 4).

What are *you* holding in *your* hand? Is it something God can use in your life as a way to serve him and others?

Best-selling author Scott Russell Sanders writes, "Over the years I have occasionally met with that union of hard work and serenity in farmers and nurses, welders and cooks, truck drivers and janitors, teachers, mechanics, letter carriers, librarians, lawyers, and clerks. These were people doing what they felt called to do, without looking for an escape, without hankering for smaller tasks or bigger paychecks....

"When I consider the varied personalities of those diligent people, I feel certain that the willingness to work hard without complaint, indeed, even with gusto, has less to do with temperament than with conviction.... If you believe that work is a calling, a discipline, a way of exercising your gifts, even a way toward God, then work will seem to you as natural, as desirable, as breathing.... The chief reason for relishing work is that it allows us to practice our faith."[5]

The Shakers, those simple, back-to-the-basics folk who are known now more for their furniture style than for the simple life they chose to follow Jesus, condensed their faith into the maxim "Hands to work, hearts to God." Thomas Merton said of them, "Love of God and love of truth in one's own work came to the same thing, and that work itself was a prayer, a communion with the inmost spiritual reality of things and so with God."[6]

Every Job Is a Ministry

What kind of job do you have? Secular or sacred? If you're a Christian, you don't have a secular job. "The ministry" is not a higher calling; it's just one of many callings. What I do on Sunday as a pastor is no more or less "spiritual" than what you do for a living. In fact, what I do could be less spiritual if I do it for the wrong reasons.

Your job is your ministry. Think about it: work is good and godly, because God worked and gave Adam work long before he sinned. And Adam's first job—gardening—wasn't "spiritual" at all. It surely was sacred, though, because it was work from God and Adam did it for God.

Work is not a curse; it's a gift from God.

When God finished Creation, everything was good, including work. But when Adam sinned, God cursed work and it became "painful toil" (Gn 3:17). God's work became work without God, and work without God is a real pain.

Sadly, as a result of the curse, work has also become our greatest source of personal identity and self-worth. Maybe that's why so many women don't feel like they have an identity, because they have not been defined by the workplace. Should women be given equal opportunity and equal pay? Absolutely. But what we do for a living and where we are in the pecking order of the labor market has become a measure of our self-worth, and that's potentially unhealthy for both men and women.

It's how we grade everyone else, too. Working for fulfillment, we climb the career ladder for more power, more income, more respect. It's a curse. Work without God becomes your god, and the more you sacrifice to become successful, the more the "god" of your work will define and control you.

The curse on work is that work has become secular, godless. Think about this: the ultimate curse is hell, the utter absence of God. Hell is utterly secular. If you think you have a "secular" job and not a "sacred" one, you may be stepping right into the consequence of the curse by ruling God out of your job.

Listen to what Paul wrote about work. See if you think he considered any work "secular."

"Slaves, obey your earthly masters with respect and fear, and with sincerity of heart, just as you would obey Christ. Obey them not only to win their favor when their eye is on you, but like slaves of Christ, doing *the will of God* from your heart. Serve wholeheartedly, as if you were serving the Lord, not men, because you know that the Lord will reward everyone for whatever good he does, whether he is slave or free" (Eph 6:5-8).

The work you're doing is "the will of God"? That sounds holy to me!

William Wilberforce, the Abe Lincoln of Great Britain, labored for the abolition of slavery until Parliament passed an antislavery law in 1807, more than fifty years before the American Civil War and the Emancipation Proclamation in

1863. Christian author Os Guinness points out that the great statesman came very close to missing his calling altogether.

"When Wilberforce came to faith ... in 1785 at the age of twenty-five, his first reaction was to throw over politics for the ministry. He thought, as millions have thought before and since, that 'spiritual' affairs are far more important than 'secular' affairs.

"Fortunately, a minister—John Newton, the converted slave trader who wrote 'Amazing Grace'—persuaded Wilberforce that God wanted him to stay in politics rather than enter the ministry. 'The Lord has raised you up for the good of the nation.'

"After much prayer and thought Wilberforce concluded that Newton was right. God was calling him to champion the liberty of the oppressed—as a Parliamentarian. 'My walk,' he wrote in his journal in 1788, 'is a public one. My business is in the world; and I must mix in the assemblies of men ... the post which Providence seems to have assigned me.'"[7]

Your work is God's gift to you to serve others and worship him. It's just as "spiritual" as your pastor's "work" on Sunday morning.

....

Creator of All Good Things: How often I get caught up in dividing my "spiritual" life from my "normal" life. Show me today how to integrate both parts into a unified whole that brings glory to your name—and attracts others to the Lord. Amen.

....

....

TEN

Misbelief 10:

What I Believe About God Is More Important Than How I Treat People

If you are offering your gift at the altar and there remember that your brother has something against you, leave your gift there in front of the altar. First go and be reconciled to your brother; then come and offer your gift.

MATTHEW 5:23-24

"It's a free country!"

That's what the man yelled rudely out of his car window. Road rage? Nope. Just another irritable Christian. The parking lot attendant had just tried to suggest to this man where he should park.

Scottsdale Bible Church is huge. About five thousand people attend every weekend, and they have a messy parking problem. Landlocked in an upscale residential area, their parking lot cannot be expanded to accommodate their enormous congregation.

So they've resorted to jamming cars, bumper to bumper, into designated parking areas. This, of course, has created problems of its own. Not every Christian can deal with inconveniences of this magnitude.

After all, it's a free country.

The pastor of Scottsdale Bible, Daryl Delhousay, told me, "We're thinking about installing flashing signs at the entrances of our parking lot: Worship Starts Here."

Send Them Home

We've had parking problems at our church too. After driving around and around looking for a spot, visitors drive away. So we have a little rule: the closer you are to God, the farther away you park from the front entrance of the worship center.

None of our church staff, myself included, has "reserved" parking.

To help people understand why they need to change their parking habits, I remind them of the story of Jesus feeding five thousand people with five buns and two fish sticks (see Mk 6:30-44). That he was able to feed so many with so little wasn't the only miracle that day. The other miracle was his getting the disciples to crawl out of their body bag of selfishness.

Overwhelmed by the crowds, the disciples reported to Jesus, "How are we going to feed all these people? It would take eight months of wages to buy all that food!" And then these followers of Jesus concluded, "Send the people away."

Send them away from Jesus? Can you believe it?

Sometimes those who are closest to Jesus keep others away. Church people almost always take the best parking places. After all, they're the ones who pay for them! So I try to get people to see that parking is a ministry. (There is a God. *Everything* matters.) When you give up your little convenience and walk a block to church, the person who takes your favorite parking slot might give his life to Christ.

We have seating problems, too, which also rankles church people. One man was *so* upset about our ushers "forcing" him to sit where he didn't want to sit that I had to step in. I laid my hand tenderly on his heart and, looking directly into his angry eyes, assured him gently, "Jesus can help you get through this. It's gonna be OK."

He said nothing. I'm not sure he still attends our church.

You Aren't Important—I Am

"It's a free country!" The sentiment is easy to translate, really: "You aren't important; I am. And I won't think twice about letting the community bleed to death on the altar of my self-interests."

Does that sound really rude? Well, an old friend once told me bitterly, "Fundamentalist Christians (those are the ones who have big Bibles) love God and hate people." It really hit me wrong. I was defensive. But over time I've come to agree with him in principle.

For all our protestations about secular humanism splattering all around us, no secular humanist has ever told me what I can or cannot preach. I've never been persecuted by a secular humanist, not in twenty-five years of ministry. But, oh boy, have I been persecuted by Christian brothers and sisters! Devout Christians in my own church.

And I'm not just talking about church squabbles. I've been flat-out betrayed. I've had long-standing relationships vanish like vapor. Staff. Elders. Friends. And in some cases, when I've made attempts to communicate with these people, I've been rebuffed. But those people keep right on going to another church somewhere, worshiping God and reading their Bibles as if nothing had ever happened. Old "friends" are forgotten as they make new ones.

As if God doesn't see through that?

Jesus taught us, "If you are offering your gift at the altar and there remember that your brother has something against you, leave your gift there in front of the altar. First go and be reconciled to your brother; then come and offer your gift" (Mt 5:23-24). I've always taken this to mean that God doesn't want our religion if it doesn't make a radical difference in the way we relate to others.

Many in our congregation come to us unchurched, but most slide in from another church, some covertly. So in our church membership seminar, one of the first things I teach our new people is how to leave one church and join another.

I insist that if they just can't bring themselves to have a personal meeting with their former pastor or leaders, they should write a gracious, appreciative letter. Tell him or her, "Thank you for the years of ministry you and your people invested in my life. The seasons of life change, and I believe God is leading me into a new church commitment. I pray for God's very best for you and your congregation."

No innuendos, please, like, "I just wasn't growing there anymore" or "If you were more open to the Holy Spirit..." or "If it were not for the one troubling person in the children's ministry...." Please leave out that junk!

Two Golden Calves

Americans—believers and unbelievers alike—have fashioned themselves not one but two golden calves. One is the pursuit of happiness. The other is individual rights. "It's a free country!" means, mostly, "I can do whatever I want and nobody's gonna stop me."

Criminals often seem to have more "rights" than victims because it's a free country. That freedom is seen in lots of other ways as well: Personal bankruptcies are at an all-time high. Road rage erupts on freeways and in church parking lots. People "church hop" among local congregations. Marriages end without regard for the welfare of the children. Millions of women, including an appalling number of Christian women, get abortions. Millions more, men and women, sleep around. Students in our public schools don't respect authority or each other.

It's a free country. And becoming freer every minute. But there's a cost, and it's a dear one.

The problems are everywhere. A recent article in a major airline's in-flight magazine, "When Less Is More," reported, "More than half of all first marriages (and 60 percent of second marriages) end in divorce—rates that are 34 percent higher than in 1970. Research indicates that 60 percent of financially successful professionals are depressed or stressed. Major surveys conclude that 48 percent of top executives claim their lives are empty or meaningless. Teen suicides, adolescent drug abuse, and high school dropout rates are rising. And although the country's Gross Domestic Product has risen steadily for the past twenty-five years, the American Index of Social Health (a figure compiled from sixteen measurable social indicators) is 52 percent lower than it was in 1973."[1]

It's a free country.

Let freedom ring.

A Cauldron of Moral Confusion

America is a cauldron of moral confusion. Volcanic cultural and social forces are reshaping everything we believe, and most of us, Christians included, are being passively poisoned. We no longer embrace a distinctively Christian, countercultural worldview. The world has baited us, and we've swallowed the hook.

A great part of the deception is that we no longer know what's "worldly," another Christian myth that keeps us chasing the wind. "Worldly" is not just smoking, drinking, dancing, and going to R-rated movies. Paul goes much deeper:

"So here's what I want you to do, God helping you: Take your everyday, ordinary life—your sleeping, eating, going-to-work, and walking-around life—and place it before God as an offering. Embracing what God does for you is the best thing you can do for him. Don't become so well-adjusted to your culture that you fit into it without even thinking. Instead, fix your attention on God. You'll be changed from the inside out. Readily recognize what he wants from you, and quickly respond to it. Unlike the culture around you, always dragging you down to its level ..., God brings the best out of you" (Rom 12:1-2, THE MESSAGE).

We Christians have adapted our faith and morals to fit secular American ideals. Allow me to walk you through the jungle of our cultural confusion. Be forewarned: you may discover that you are more worldly than you think.

Jesus and Me and the Community

Let's study carefully that second golden calf: individualism.

Communism holds that the individual is worthless, except as he or she fits into the system and serves the needs of the state. On the other hand, our American democracy values and protects individual rights, often at the expense of the community good. What is the biblical perspective?

In the Bible, God affirms both the community and the individual. Each of us is uniquely created and gifted by God, but our individuality has no meaning outside of the community.

The apostle Paul wrote, "The eye cannot say to the hand, 'I don't need you!' And the head cannot say to the feet, 'I don't need you!' On the contrary, those parts of the body that seem to be weaker are indispensable" (1 Cor 12:21-22).

Each member of my body has a special form and function,

but rip it out of my body and it's just dead meat. This is interdependence, as opposed to dependence (only the community matters, communism) and independence (only the individual matters, "this is a free country").

The whole planet is an interdependent system. Somehow along the food chain I depend on algae. Everything in the ecosystem is necessary (although some have suggested that the earth would get along just fine without people!). Do you know who's responsible for all this interdependence? Would it be God?

Look at Genesis 1:26-27: "God said, 'Let us make man in our image, in our likeness, and let them rule over the fish of the sea and the birds of the air, over the livestock, over all the earth, and over all the creatures that move along the ground.'

"So God created man in his own image, in the image of God he created him; male and female he created them."

The Triune God is an interdependent community within himself. That's his image, and that's what he's created in us. God said, "Let *us* create man in *our* image." God's image is not in me; it's in my relationships with others; it's in the whole community.

In the original Hebrew language of the Old Testament, the last three lines of the Genesis passage above are themselves interdependent,[2] that is, they build on one another, which tells us that "the image of God" is in the interdependent community and diversity of "male and female."

The other commonly used biblical image of interdependence, as I've already noted, is the body of Christ. I especially like this verse: "God has arranged the parts in the body, every one of them, just as he wanted them to be" (1 Cor 12:18). Paul isn't giving us an anatomy lesson. He's talking about people, difficult people, unwanted people. No relationship is accidental, unless you're an evolutionist who believes that the controlling principle of the universe is chance.

Christians have to believe, because there's a God, that every relationship is purposeful. According to the verse above, no one just walks into your life without God having some reason for it, or at the very least, without your having something to learn from it.

Life's a Package

When my father died last December, my youngest brother took it much harder than we expected. We had talked a lot about our feelings and why this was so difficult. David said to me reflectively, "It's because life is a package. We're the sum of all our relationships, and Dad was such a huge part of that."

No one is an island. We are who we are because of a myriad of relationships, both good and bad. Now, that doesn't mean that I can't help who I am, but I am defined by all the people in my life. It's what philosopher-theologian Martin Buber referred to as "I-Thou." Without you, I'm nothing.

The Cult of the Individual

In America it is the individual that thrives, not the community. Author Scott Russell Sanders refers to the problem as "the cult of the individual." In his delicious book, *Writing from the Center,* Sanders laments the absence of community in American values.

"The cult of the individual shows up everywhere in American lore, which celebrates drifters, rebels, and loners, while pitying or reviling the pillars of the community. The backwoods explorer like Daniel Boone,... the daring crook like Jesse James and the resourceful killer like Billy the Kid, along with countless lonesome cowboys, all wander, unattached, through the greatest spaces of our imagination.

"When society begins to close in, making demands and asking questions, our heroes hit the road. Like Huckleberry Finn, they are forever lighting out for the Territory, where nobody will tell them what to do."[3]

Nearly thirty years ago, popular and influential writer, Alvin Toffler, diagnosed the American problem still another way in his classic book on trends, *Future Shock*. Urbanization, he said, is a principal cause of the end of community. Oddly, more people crammed together in smaller spaces does not make for more community. More people means more madness.

And along with bigger cities, more trash. Toffler coined the phrase "a throw-away generation." You know what else we've learned to throw away? People. Toffler had a term for that too: "modular relationships." He meant that we connect and disconnect from other people like a plug and a wall socket. When we need something, we plug in. When we don't need it anymore, we unplug. No love lost.

If the service at a restaurant isn't meeting our expectations, we don't go back. If the shoe salesman doesn't wait on us quickly, we're outraged and report it to his supervisor. Never mind that his wife left him the night before. If a pastor says or does something that offends us, never mind if it's petty, we just leave the church in a huff.

It's a free country.

My needs come first.

An Epidemic of Loneliness

People have been talking about the crisis of community in America for decades. Almost as long ago as Toffler wrote *Future Shock*, sociologist Ralph Keyes authored *We the Lonely People*. I've never read a better analysis of why America has gone bad—and why the mission of the church has never been more necessary and more difficult.

"Community," Keyes wrote, "is a national obsession. But we want other things more. Not getting involved with the neighbors is worth more to us than 'community.' ... It's this confusion, this ambivalence, that confounds our quest for community. We yearn for a simpler, more communal life; we sincerely want more sense of community. But not at the sacrifice of any advantages that mass society has brought, even ones we presumably scorn.

"We didn't lose community. We bought it off.... I could find a mom and pop store if I really wanted one. But I don't. I prefer a supermarket's prices and selection. Also the anonymity, the fact that I'm not burdened by knowing the help.... We crave anonymity. And rather than take paths that might lead us back together, we pursue the very things that keep us cut off from each other."[4]

Why are we so lonely? What are the enemies of friendship and community? What are "the very things that keep us cut off from one another"? Keyes suggests four.

1. The 'M-Factor'

In 1849 Scottish journalist Alexander McKay wrote, "How readily an American makes up his mind to try his fortunes elsewhere." Called the "M-factor"—movement, migration, and mobility—it's what has shaped our national character.

As Americans, we've even found that there's a direct relationship between mobility and success. You've got to move to get a better job. I did.

Mobility is an enemy of friendship. But are we afraid to get close because we're always moving on, or are we always moving on because we're afraid to get close?

2. I Want to Be Alone

Tell me, do you value your privacy? I love my privacy, but writing this chapter makes me think I should feel a little guilty for loving my privacy so much. Privacy as an ideal, as a concept, is relatively modern. I hate to say this, but privacy is not really Christian. Did you know that neither the Japanese nor the Arabs even have an exact word for privacy? And it's almost impossible to find the concept in the Bible?

John McKay, former head football coach at USC and later of the L.A. Rams, once was heard to say, "The neighbors are perfect. I don't know any of them."

3. The Downside of Convenience

Many modern appliances and conveniences—dishwashers, microwaves, fast food—have drastically reduced the amount of time many families spend on chores. While that may not seem like a bad thing at first, it does have a down side: We don't have many chores to do, so we don't do them together.

Sit-down family dinners are a thing of the past. We don't relate; we don't interact; we hardly even communicate. As an antidote to this social poison, best-selling Christian author and conference speaker Gary Smalley recommends a radical approach to building family communication, interaction, and values: camping. Camping doesn't allow mobility, privacy, or convenience!

4. On the Road Alone

Watch car ads thoughtfully. What are they selling? Transportation? Or is it more about image and personal comfort and privacy? Think about the individualism in every ad: the lonely driver on a lonely road. Never do you see car ads filmed on freeways, except when they want to show you someone leaving the freeway, getting away from it all. For Europeans, the automobile is for transportation. For Americans, it's an escape.

Ralph Keyes writes, "Cars and bathrooms are the only places

where most urban-suburbanites can be completely and blissfully alone. And a car is better than the bathroom. No one can knock and tell you to hurry up."[5]

Koinonia, Shared Life

When you give your life to Jesus, it means you join his body. You become an interdependent participant in the Christian community. As a result of the great outpouring of the Holy Spirit at Pentecost, three thousand people were saved. "They devoted themselves," Luke reports in the Book of Acts, "to the apostles' teaching and to the fellowship [Greek: *koinonia,* 'shared life'], to the breaking of bread and to prayer" (Acts 2:42).

This Bible text doesn't say that the early Christians devoted themselves to God, although they certainly did that. This verse in Acts, though, tells us they devoted themselves to one another.

Does this sound alien? Generally, we think of devotion in the context of religious practices. For the early church, devotion was inseparable from the community of the believers. How devoted to one another were they? "All the believers were together and had everything in common [Greek: *koine,* same basic term used in verse 42]" (v. 44).

Borrowing from Rick Warren's book *The Purpose Driven Church,* we've defined official membership at our church as, among other things, "being as committed to one another as we are to Jesus Christ." Do you bolt at that? Think of the words of the apostle John: "If anyone says, 'I love God,' yet hates his brother, he is a liar. For anyone who does not love his brother, whom he has seen, cannot love God, whom he has not seen" (1 Jn 4:20).

The Bible on Tolerance

Being a Christian doesn't mean that we've just become a little more tolerant, because Jesus helps us love people we don't like. Sometimes when my Christian brothers and sisters have learned how to put up with somebody, they feel they've made huge strides towards Christlikeness. But nowhere in the Bible are we instructed to "tolerate" differences.

Hold on to your seat, now: the teaching of the Bible is that real Christians *value* the differences and difficulties in relationships, because they afford a greater opportunity for us to become more like Jesus. I don't need Jesus to endure the occasional oddities of generally likable people. Jesus said, "Even 'sinners' do that" (Lk 6:33).

It's the most difficult people in the most difficult circumstances that both test and deepen my faith. Jesus adds, "But love your enemies, do good to them, and lend to them without expecting to get anything back. Then your reward will be great, and you will be sons of the Most High, because he is kind to the ungrateful and wicked" (v. 35).

In a brief editorial, "Why I Attend a Small Church," author Philip Yancey says it simply: "because I can't choose my own friends." In a small church God picks your friends, because you know everybody, and you have to include everybody, love everybody, and do the best you can to get along with everybody.

In a big church in a big city, people hide. And when we find them, they run. We're trying to change that in our congregation ... but then we can hardly get people to put up with a parking inconvenience.

After all, this is a free country!

....

Holy Liberator: How can we compare your eternal riches to our small conveniences? How could we exchange our small liberties for the glory of your body, the church? Give me a fresh vision for how you want to draw me closer to yourself—and to my brothers and sisters around me. Amen.

....

....

ELEVEN

Misbelief 11:

Reality Is Not What You Think:
Four Ways to Change Your Thoughts for Good

> Do not conform any longer to the pattern of this
> world, but be transformed by the renewing of your
> mind.
>
> ROMANS 12:2

Well, you've made it this far. It's the last chapter in our journey together.

If I made you angry, at least you kept reading your way through the book. You know, some people won't let you finish a sentence! I'm very grateful you're finishing this book.

And thank you for thinking. And rethinking.

We're back to the reason I wrote this book: to help you break through the barriers of popular misbeliefs and to think biblically about God, yourself, and others. Change your thoughts and you'll change your life!

Recently, the national media reported remarkable advances in brain chemistry research. Scientists have discovered that changing the way you think actually changes the way the brain functions. Studies have shown that extended psychoanalysis and counseling, for example, alter the chemistry of the brain and, consequently, a person's behaviors.

If that's true of "secular" therapy, think about the potential impact of daily time in the Word of God, frequent prayer, exposure to the presence and power of the Holy Spirit, and quality time with godly people!

Think about that!

If reality isn't what you think, then you need to change what you think. In this last chapter, then, let me walk you through a process of self-discovery and healing.

Nobody Makes You Mad

I have on the desk next to me an ancient little book, *Why I'm Afraid to Tell You Who I Am,* by John Powell. Published in the 1960s, this book's cover is psychedelic purple. But the contents are timeless. And it's had a significant impact on my life because it's forced me to think about what I think.

In one part of the book Powell writes, "The syndicated columnist, Sydney Harris, tells the story of accompanying his friend to a newsstand. The friend greeted the newsman very courteously, but in return received gruff and discourteous service. Accepting the newspaper which was shoved rudely in his direction, the friend of Harris politely smiled and wished the newsman a nice weekend. As the two friends walked down the street, the columnist asked:

"'Does he always treat you so rudely?'

"'Yes, unfortunately he does.'

"'And are you always so polite and friendly to him?'

"'Yes, I am.'

"'Why are you so nice to him when he is so unfriendly to you?'

"'Because I don't want *him* to decide how *I'm* going to act.'

"The suggestion is that the 'fully human' person ... does not bend to every wind which blows, that he is not at the mercy of all the pettiness, the meanness, the impatience and anger of others. Atmospheres do not transform him as much as he transforms them."[1]

You Make You Mad

The people and pressures in my life don't make me depressed; something inside me makes me depressed. In an earlier chapter I acknowledged the dark side of my soul, and I told you how I can be depressed when there isn't a reason in the world to be depressed. Although my darkness deepens in difficult times, mostly my depression is inside me.

Reality is not what happens to me but what I think about what happens to me. We have little or no control over what happens *to* us, but God's grace gives us more control over what happens *in* us than we are willing to admit and accept. You *can* control yourself, and it has to do with what you think.

One evening, a few years back, my wife, Marilyn, and I were having a less-than-cordial exchange of personal opinion. I think it was about something really important, like wallpaper. Just then the doorbell rang. I took a deep breath, put on a mask of self-composure, and opened the door. I was hoping for a salesman so I could get right back to our argument.

But it was my brother, paying me an entirely unexpected visit, standing there and looking at me with a suspicious grin. It was that kind of look that said, "I've been listening through the door to you and Marilyn fighting." In fact, Tom had no idea anything out of the ordinary was going on inside the house. I just imagined that he knew.

I'll never forget how my feelings changed, almost instantly. Almost miraculously. Inside my stormy soul I wanted to keep on being angry, but I couldn't. Really, I tried, but when my brother smiled at me, I smiled back. As my thoughts changed, my angry emotions subsided. Marilyn and I never resumed the fight. At least not that one.

My wife didn't make me angry; I made me angry. What I was thinking made me angry, and when I changed what I was thinking, I stopped being angry. Reality is not what happens to me but what I think about what happens to me.

Let me demonstrate that to you another way. Think about one of the most painful moments in your past. What was it? Think about it. Tell me about it. I bet you can't without your feelings of anger and resentment bleeding through. What you think determines how you feel, not the other way around.

Earlier this afternoon, as I was reviewing and editing the story of Jeff and Kathy in chapter eight, I started to sob. Kathy's death occurred two years ago, but when I think about it, all my emotions begin to resurface. You know, that's how an actress cries real tears in a movie, or even live on stage. That's right, by thinking about something sad in her own life.

Not What Happened to You,
But What You Think Happened to You

Men are not worried by things, but by their ideas about things. When we meet with difficulties, become anxious and troubled, let us not blame others, but rather ourselves; that is, our ideas about things.

EPICTETUS

Almost all our misfortunes in life come from the wrong notions we have about the things that happen to us.

MARIE STENDHAL

It's not what happens to you. It's what happens *in* you.

JOHN MAXWELL

The Hebrew prophet Ezekiel heard God say, "Son of man, hast thou seen what the ancients of the house of Israel do in the dark, every man in the chambers of his imagery?" (Ez 8:12, KJV). This verse refers to literal idolatry in ancient Israel, a persistent sin that led to the eventual destruction of the Jewish nation.

But this Scripture also has a profound application to the theme of this chapter. Tell me, what's going on in *your* mind? What's happening in the "chambers of your imagery"? What's going on in the secret imaginations of your heart, and how is that damaging your life?

Before we move on to the four ways you can change your

thoughts for good, allow me to introduce you to a famous psychologist by the name of Albert Ellis, who based his model of therapy on the idea that personal problems are the result of irrational belief systems or patterns of thought. Called the rational-emotive (thinking-feeling) model of human behavior, it goes something like this:

$$A \longrightarrow B \longrightarrow C$$

A is the "Actuating Event," or what happens to you.

B is your "Belief," or what you think about what happens to you.

C is the "Consequence," what you end up doing or feeling about what you think about what happened to you.

Now here's how most of us relate to people and problems. We take no time to think about what we're thinking, like this:

$$A \longrightarrow C$$

We skip right over B (we're thinking about A) and blurt out irrationalities like "That person makes me so angry," or "You really get to me," or "Her remark embarrassed me terribly," or "This weather really depresses me," or "This job really bores me," or "The very sight of him makes me want to cry."[2]

Without a second thought (and that's the problem!), we leap from A to C. But there's a consequential factor between A and C. Me!

$$A \longrightarrow B \text{ (me)} \longrightarrow C$$

If You Are Going to Live Well, You Must Live by the Truth

Reality is not what happens to me (A) but what I think about what happens to me (B). Did you know this is a thoroughly biblical principle? It's stated this way: "We live by faith, not by sight" (2 Cor 5:7).

"Faith" is what we believe and think, what happens *in* us. "Sight" is what we see and hear, what happens *to* us. Ultimate reality for the Christian is what she believes, not what she sees. Check out these other Bible verses, and see how they support this thinking-feeling model of human behavior:

- "Immediately the rooster crowed the second time. Then Peter remembered the word Jesus had spoken to him: 'Before the rooster crows twice you will disown me three times.' And he broke down and wept" (Mk 14:72).
- "By the rivers of Babylon we sat and wept when we remembered Zion" (Ps 137:1).
- "I remember my affliction and my wandering, the bitterness and the gall. I will remember them, and my soul is downcast within me. Yet this I call to mind and therefore I have hope:

    "Because of the Lord's great love we are not consumed, for his compassions never fail. They are new every morning; great is your faithfulness. I say to myself, 'The Lord is my portion; therefore I will wait for him'" (Lam 3:19-24).
- "For the weapons of our warfare are ... mighty through God ... casting down imaginations, and every high thing that exalteth itself against the knowledge of God, and bringing into captivity every thought to the obedience of Christ" (2 Cor 10:4-5, KJV).

Based on the Bible, here's how I propose to modify Ellis' model of human behavior:

The Cross

A ———> me ———> C

The Holy Spirit

I am powerless to change the way I think, because my mind is bound by the law of sin and death. I can't change me, no matter how hard I try. The pure power of positive thinking can help a little, but it can't change what's in my heart. I am compelled to bow down to idols in the chambers of my imagery. Only my dying to self (me under the cross) and the help of the Holy Spirit (the Holy Spirit holding me up) will enable me to change my old pattern of thinking and empower me to think the thoughts that will change my life.

The apostle Paul is on to this in Galatians 5:16-18: "I say, live by the Spirit, and you will not gratify the desires of the sinful nature. For the sinful nature desires what is contrary to the Spirit, and the Spirit what is contrary to the sinful nature. They are in conflict with each other, so that you do not do what you want [I am powerless]. But if you are led by the Spirit, you are not under law [the futility of human effort, the curse of the curve]."

Four Ways to Change Your Thoughts for Good

Let's review.

Nobody makes you mad.

You make you mad.

It's not what happens to you; it's what you think about what happens to you.

To live well, you have to learn to live by the truth. You need to change your thoughts for good: "Do not conform any longer to the pattern of this world, but be transformed by the renewing of your mind" (Rom 12:2).

How do you renew your mind? How do you change your thoughts for good? There are four catalysts.

1. The Big Turnaround

Wrong thinking is a sin problem, and so the solution lies in repentance. You begin the process of change by acknowledging your misbeliefs, confessing them to God, and confessing them to someone who can pray for you (see 1 Jn 1:8-9).

Repentance, unfortunately, has come to refer to a religious experience, and generally people have no idea what the word actually means. The New Testament Greek word for "repent" means, literally, "to change your mind." One very scholarly resource in my personal library defines repentance as "a radical acknowledgment of God ... as well as a radical confession of sinful falleness."[3]

Eons ago, before the Great Flood of Noah, the Bible records that "the Lord saw how great man's wickedness on the earth had become, and that every inclination of the thoughts of his heart was only evil all the time" (Gn 6:5). Centuries later the apostle Paul was still singing the same sad song: "Although they knew God, they neither glorified him as God nor gave thanks to him, but their thinking became futile and their foolish hearts were darkened" (Rom 1:21).

Wrong thinking is a sin problem.

2. Bread for the Brain

The Bible has the power to change your thoughts for two essential reasons: (1) it's God Word, and (2) it's the truth. As God's Word, the Bible is much more than a record of things people thought about God.

The Bible has an energy of its own, for it is the Word of God. It's not just a book of good things to think about. It has the power literally to change your thoughts when you are powerless.

Paul knew this when he wrote to Timothy that the Scriptures are "God-breathed" (2 Tm 3:16). This blows right by us today, but for Paul, in his setting, the term "God-breathed" reached back to the opening chapters of the Bible, where it is recorded that God breathed into man the breath of life, and man became a living soul (see Gn 2:7). As human persons are created in the image of God and share in God's life, so the Bible is infused with the life-giving breath and Spirit of God. The power of the Scriptures is the power of the Holy Spirit working in and through God's Word.

Both Hebrew and Greek words for "breath" also mean "spirit." In a clever play on words, Jesus interfaces these ideas of breath and spirit and life: "The Spirit gives life; the flesh counts for nothing. The words I have spoken to you are spirit and they are life" (Jn 6:63).

The Word of God is, indeed, "living and active. Sharper than any double-edged sword, it penetrates even to dividing soul and spirit, joints and marrow; it judges the thoughts and attitudes of the heart" (Heb 4:12). It's powerful! That's why Jesus confronted the very devil himself with Scripture: "It is written: 'Man does not live on bread alone, but on every word that comes from the mouth of God'" (Mt 4:4).

The Bible is bread for your brain!

To put the Bible to work for you, especially when you are struggling with deeply entrenched, self-destructive thought patterns, I suggest you become a card-carrying Christian. I'm indebted to best-selling author Norm Wright for this idea. It's simple: take a three-by-five-inch card, and on one side write down the Scripture or Scriptures you find especially life-giving for your personal situation. On the other side, write "STOP!" in large letters.

Carry the card with you. When your thoughts start running away from you, pull out the card and read it to yourself (out loud, if you can). Say it to yourself: "STOP!" Tell your brain, "Stop thinking that way!" Then turn the card over and review the Bible references. Read them again and again, many times a day if it's necessary. I'm telling you this because it's helped me big-time. I lived on Psalm 20:1-5 for nearly a year.

The Bible has a word for this kind of mental exercise: "meditation." Meditation is medication for your thought life, for your soul: "I remember the days of long ago; I meditate on all your works and consider what your hands have done. I spread out my hands to you; my soul thirsts for you like a parched land. *Selah* [which means, think about this even more]" (Ps 143:5-6).

3. Power Thoughts Through the Holy Spirit

I've done extensive study and writing on the subject of spiritual warfare, and I've concluded that our minds interface daily with the spiritual realm.[4]

Whether or not you believe it, whether or not you think about it consciously, it's a matter of fact that you have ears to hear and eyes to see something of what is on the other side of time and space. Created in the image of God, human persons have a deep spiritual capacity. The chemistry of the human brain is more than chemicals. You can connect with God. And angels.

And the devil?

Paul warns us about this: "I am afraid that just as Eve was deceived by the serpent's cunning, your minds may somehow be led astray from your sincere and pure devotion to Christ" (2 Cor 11:3). This is the war zone in your head, and it's why Paul commands Christians to put on the full armor of God, including the helmet of salvation for your head, because "our struggle is not against flesh and blood, but against the rulers, against the authorities, against the powers of this dark world and against the spiritual forces of evil in the heavenly realms" (Eph 6:12).

What you think is not always you. Sometimes it's a power encounter with evil, and the real presence of God is necessary to protect your mind and to empower you to believe and obey the Word of God.

Which brings us to our utter dependence on the third and most powerful of the four ways to change your thoughts for good: the Holy Spirit, who is the Third Person of God himself. "I will ask the Father," Jesus promised, "and he will give you another Counselor to be with you forever—the Spirit of truth" (Jn 14:16-17).

4. When It Hurts to Think

Last, but you're going to like this least, the fourth way to change your thoughts is, well, something you can't make happen. It's completely out of your control: crisis.

One of the great misbeliefs of the church is the widespread assumption that if you go to Sunday service, if someone preaches or teaches God's Word to you, you will change. Yes, God's Word is infused with intrinsic power, and faith comes by hearing the Word of God (see Rom 10:17). But the reality is that people don't change because they hear the truth or read good Christian books. Oh, maybe they do a little, but the changes they make are more like adjustments. Sometimes my car needs a tune-up. Sometimes it needs a new engine, like when the first one blows up.

People change radically when the hurricanes of life blow through their brains. Just talking about change changes people only slightly—for the simple reason that significant change hurts too much. Generally people won't change unless the pain to stay the same becomes greater than the pain to change.

My basic personality has stayed pretty much the same for the last twenty years, but I sure mellowed out in the late 1980s. In a personal crisis of reality my life was marked forever. I am like

Jacob, who after spending a dark and mysterious night wrestling with an angel, came away from the ford of the Jabbok with a permanently dislocated hip and a new name, Israel.

I'm still basically the same guy I was twenty years ago, but people close to me would tell you that I'm a different man. God didn't change my name, like Jacob, but I have a heart arrhythmia. Every time I experience a PVC (that's short for preventricular contraction)—and I can feel every single one—I hear the voice of God. Sort of like Paul, I can say that I bear on my body the marks of the Lord Jesus (see Gal 6:17). My heart problem is a constant reminder that Jesus is Lord of everything and I'm lord of nothing.

I would never want to relive those desperate years again, not for a million bucks. Yet they're a priceless treasure in my life, because I could not be who I am today without that crisis, without that pain. I had to change, because the pain to stay the same was killing me.

I wish it were different, but hardship is the way the Lord disciplines us: "My son, do not make light of the Lord's discipline, and do not lose heart when he rebukes you, because the Lord disciplines those he loves, and he punishes everyone he accepts as a son. Endure hardship as discipline" (Heb 12:5-7). Which is why James offers his infamous invitation to "consider it pure joy ... whenever you face trials of many kinds" (Jas 1:2). Doesn't that just make you gnash your teeth?

I like the way J.B. Phillips renders this: "When all kinds of troubles crowd into your lives, my brothers, don't resent them as intruders, but welcome them as friends! Realize that they come to test your faith and to produce in you the quality of endurance. But let the process go on until that endurance is fully developed, and you will find you have become people of mature character, people of integrity with no weak spots" (Jas 1:2-4, *The New Testament in Modern English*).

Have You Suffered Enough?

It's the mature Christian who can welcome adversity as an opportunity to look at himself more deeply and to reach out to God more fervently. So if you made it all the way through this book without a whimper, without a breath of protest, then I haven't done my job. If this book hasn't made you suffer even slightly, then it probably hasn't changed the way you think much at all.

You see, I've prayed that this book would, well, provoke you. Not to anger but to good works. Besides, if after reading this chapter, you howl something like "This book makes me so mad," it would just make you look foolish.

I've also prayed that this book would set you free from the misery of common misbeliefs and deepen your love for God and your appreciation for his utterly unconditional grace.

Is God answering my prayer?

NOTES

....

INTRODUCTION
Smart Reasons to Read This Book

1. David G. Myers, *The Inflated Self: Human Illusions and the Biblical Call to Hope* (New York: Seabury, 1980), 22–24.
2. Chris Thurman, *The Lies We Believe: The #1 Cause of Our Happiness* (Nashville: Thomas Nelson, 1989), 22–24.

ONE
Misbelief 1:
God Is Eternal, But Mostly I Worry About What He Thinks of Me Now

1. A.W. Tozer, *The Knowledge of the Holy* (New York: Harper & Row, 1961), 9–13.
2. Steve McVey, *Grace Walk* (Eugene, Ore.: Harvest House, 1996), 18.
3. I've often heard people say that this happens when we pray in tongues, but the context has nothing to do with speaking in tongues. Quite clearly here, the Spirit intercedes for us (Greek: *anti*, or "instead of us") with groanings "words cannot express." Speaking in tongues may sound like groaning, but it's still something that requires the expression of words. The groans of the Holy Spirit in intercession for us are silent.

TWO
Misbelief 2:
God Is Nit-Picking and Short-Tempered

1. I believe in the historic Christian position on the Godhead, that God is Trinity, but frankly it's not an easy doctrine to explain. The nature of Christ and his relationship to the Father was, in fact, one of the most controversial issues in the first few hundred years of Christian history. Around A.D. 1000 the church suffered its first major division, which had to do with, among other things, a slight difference on how to define the Trinity.

    Certainly issues of power and control were part of it, but the final straw was a theological argument over the Latin word *filioque*, which means "and the Son." The creed of the Eastern Orthodox Church reads, "I believe in the Holy Spirit, who proceeds from the Father." You are probably more familiar with the Western creed: "I believe in the Holy Spirit, who proceeds from the Father and the Son." That last phrase is the English translation of the original Latin term, *filioque*. A thousand years removed, it's hard for us to imagine why *filioque* was such a big deal, but then why is your issue right now such a big deal?

THREE
Misbelief 3:
God Grades on a Curve
(The Better You Are, the Bigger the Blessing)

1. George Barna, "What Effective Churches Have Discovered," seminar.
2. George Barna, *Index of Leading Spiritual Indicators* (Dallas: Word, 1996), 71.
3. Henri Nouwen, *The Return of the Prodigal Son: A Story of Homecoming* (New York: Doubleday, 1994), 42–43.

FOUR
Misbelief 4:
God Is Love, So He'll Overlook What I'm Doing

1. George Barna, "The American Witness," *The Barna Report*, November/December 1997, 3.
2. Greek *aphiemi*, which means "I release."
3. Philip Yancey, "The Unmoral Prophets," *Christianity Today*, October 5, 1998, 76.
4. Yancey, 77.
5. Richard Dawkins, as quoted in Yancey, 77.
6. Stewart Vogel, as quoted in Terry Mattingly, "Thou Shalt Listen Closely," *The Arizona Republic*, September 26, D4.
7. James Dobson, *Focus on the Family Newsletter*, April 1993, 3.
8. John Kohan, "The New Russian Culture: A Mind of Their Own," *Time*, December 7, 1992, 68.
9. Yuri Zarakhovich, "A Russian's Lament: Democracy Must Mean Much More Than Sausage," *Time*, September 21, 1998, 76.

10. Marianne K. Hering, "Believe Well, Live Well," *Focus on the Family Newsletter,* September 1994, 4.

11. Carol Tavris and Susan Sadd, *The Redbook Report on Female Sexuality* (New York: Delacorte Press, 1977), 3.

12. Judith Wallerstein and Sandra Blakeslee, *Second Chances: Men, Women, and Children a Decade After Divorce* (New York: Ticknor & Fields, 1990).

13. Thomas Schmidt, *Straight and Narrow?* (Downers Grove, Ill.: InterVarsity Press, 1995); and "Homosexuality and Christian Morality," an audiocassette available from the Veritas Forum, 1-800-2-REASON.

14. Hering, 3.

15. Rebecca A. Clay, "Psychologists' Faith in Religion Begins to Grow," *The APA Monitor,* Vol. 27, No. 8, August 1996, 1ff.

16. Joyce Brothers, in an article featured in *New Woman,* June 1995.

17. "Evil desire" here is misleading. In the Greek text it's just "strong desire" or "passion," something that's "just human."

18. "Pervert the gospel" is what Paul uses for any teaching that suggests our eternal relationship with God is based on Jesus plus something. See Galatians 1:6-9.

19. Frank Koch, *Proceedings,* as cited in Steven Covey, *Seven Habits of Highly Effective People* (New York: Simon & Schuster, 1989), 33.

FIVE

Misbelief 5:
God Wants Me to Be Happy;
He Will Always Protect Me From Pain and Suffering

1. *Marriage in America: A Report to the Nation* (New York: Institute for American Values, March 1995), 3, 8, italics mine. Copies of this report can be obtained by contacting Institute for American Values, 1841 Broadway, Suite 211, New York, NY 10023. Telephone (212) 246-3942.

2. Robert Wuthnow, as quoted in Donald McCullough, *The Trivialization of God: The Dangerous Illusion of a Manageable Diety* (Colorado Springs, Colo.: NavPress, 1995), 41.

3. Dan Wakefield, as quoted in McCullough, 46.

4. "Americans Begin Fifth Year as Captives," *Charisma,* March 1998, 16–17.

SEVEN

Misbelief 7:
If I Pray Enough and Work on It,
Someday My Problem Will Go Away

1. Dwight Carlson, "Exposing the Myth That Christians Should Not Have Emotional Problems," *Christianity Today*, February 3, 1998, 30.
2. Carlson, 30.

NINE

Misbelief 9:
Being Spiritual Is All That Matters,
Because It's All That Matters to God

1. This is a Greek word that referred to the captain or helmsman of a ship and to organization or directorship in the local church. J.B. Phillips, in *The New Testament in Modern English*, renders this "organizers and helpers."
2. Henry Blackaby and Claude King, *The Power of the Call* (Nashville, Tenn.: Broadman, 1997), 27.
3. Os Guinness, *The Call: Finding and Fulfilling the Central Purpose of Your Life* (Nashville, Tenn.: Word, 1998), 32–33.
4. Guinness, 34.
5. Scott Russell Sanders, *Writing from the Center* (Bloomington, Ind.: University of Indiana Press, 1995), 89–95.
6. Thomas Merton, as cited in Sanders, 96.
7. Guinness, 28–29.

TEN

Misbelief 10:
What I Believe About God
Is More Important Than How I Treat People

1. Andy Dappen, "When Less Is More," *Hemispheres*, November 1997, 155.
2. This is called a "Hebrew parallelism."
3. Sanders, 72–73.
4. Ralph Keyes, *We the Lonely People* (New York: Harper & Row, 1973), 12–13.
5. Keyes, 43.

ELEVEN
Reality Is Not What You Think:
Four Ways to Change Your Thoughts for Good

1. John Powell, *Why I'm Afraid to Tell You Who I Am* (Chicago: Peacock, 1969), 38–39.
2. Powell, 38–39.
3. Horst Balz and Gerhard Schneider, eds., *The Exegetical Dictionary of the New Testament,* vol. 2 (Grand Rapids, Mich.: Eerdmans, 1991), 417.
4. If you want to read about this in depth, I recommend my book *How to Overcome the Darkness,* published by Baker/Chosen Books.